MAN, The Superhuman

MAN, The Superhuman

A Global Prospect of Expounding Sri Aurobindo's Integral Vision of Humanity

Volume - III

Santi Nath Chattopadhyay

GYAN

First Published, 2017

Published by

Gyan Publishing House
5, Ansari Road
Daryaganj, New Delhi-110002
Phone: 9811692060
E-mail: books@gyanbooks.com

Printed at: G. Print Process, Delhi.

Cataloging in Publication Data—DK
Courtesy: D.K. Agencies (P) Ltd. <docinfo@dkagencies.com>

Chattopadhyay, Santinath, author.
Man, the super human : a global prospect of expounding Sri Aurobindo's integral vision of humanity / Santi Nath Chattopadhyay.
pages cm
Includes bibliographical references.
ISBN 9788121213547

1. Ghose, Aurobindo, 1872-1950. 2. Philosophical anthropology. 3. Humanism. I. Title.

B5134.G46C43 2017 DDC 144 23

Dedicated To

Sri Aurobindo

In Centenary Celebration of the day of His Entering into the Spiritual Life

Contents

Preface

The object of this volume is to expound Sri Aurobindo's ideas and ideals of Man, The Super Human which is not unnatural or supernatural expansion of human existence but it explores the creative potency of universality in man in expanding his universal existence as inauguration of Man as Superhuman.

It may be noted in this context that Sri Aurobindo's philosophy of Man is a result of a continuous process in dealing with socio-cultural, philosophical and religious experiences of Sri Aurobindo from a creative humanistic viewpoint in relation to the development of the universal nature of Man as Superhuman. This idea of Sri Aurobindo is associated with views of universality and spirituality, expounded by Swami Vivekananda, Rabindranath Tagore, Mahatma Gandhi, Dr Radhakrishnan and other contemporary Indian thinkers. The work is very much critical, comparative and reflective study in the form of modern evaluation of man and human existence from East-West perspectives.

Present work is also closely associated with ideas and objectives of our society-ISISAR (International Society for Intercultural Studies and Research) which like Sri Aurobindo, expounds the creative dimension of the term 'Culture'. Firstly, it means the acceptance of all Cultures, Faiths, Communities, Disciplines of the world. Secondly, 'Culture' means Cultivation of Universal value as Universal Good through the intercommunication of ideas and values in expanding intercultural relation and understanding with a prospect of developing 'World Union' as suggested by Sri Aurobindo.

In this background, it may be stated that the idea of religion as examined by Sri Aurobindo, centres round the cultural harmony in representing the essential expression of integral human outlook. This idea is intimately related with the evolution of human nature or human culture towards the eternal manifestation of perfection in realising freedom for the introduction of divinity in human life and culture. This humanistic process, according to Sri Aurobindo, is an expansion of universality which in his observation, leads to divine unity as the expression of Superhuman nature and idea in human existence. This essential and harmonious development of human nature and existence is an insightful observation of Sri Aurobindo who finally emphasis the expansion of 'Divine Life' on earth.

In the context of this brief analysis, it may be stated that the entire work on Sri Aurobindo is divided into four chapters with some parts in expounding the global prospect of Sri Aurobindo's integral vision of humanity.

To continue my extensive research, I have taken the guidance and directions of different scholars under University of Calcutta, Rabindra Bharati University, Jadavpur University, Pondicherry University and Sri Aurobindo Ashrama, Pondicherry and so I am thankful to the authorities there in stitutions.

In preparation of this work I also acknowledge the guidance from scholars on Sri Aurobindo and different types of assistance from the members of our Society-ISISAR.

I have quoted several observations of Sri Aurobindo from different English writings, but so far as Bengali writings are concerned I have tried to translate these into English. If there is any fault, it will be ignored for consideration.

The glory of the work is extended through its FOREWORD, written by Dr Glen T. Martin, Professor of Philosophy, Religion and Peace Studies, Radford University, USA, who has expressed his modern view points through his insightful writings. I express my heartfelt thanks and gratefulness to him for expanding his stimulating ideas and outlook in the FOREWORD on the theme of the volume.

In the preparation of the work I gratefully acknowledge the guidance and assistance of Dr Rajesh Rastogi, Delhi University,

Professor Maniklal Bandyopadhyay, Professor Chhanda Chatterjee, Dr Sudipto Chatterjee, Smt Somdutta Chatterjee, Sri Ram Krishna Mondal and other members of ISISAR.

I take the opportunity to thank my publisher Gyan Publication House, New Delhi for bringing out the volume.

Finally, I may state that I shall be richly rewarded if my venture of developing 'Trilogy' in expanding the creative and the constructive ideas of Man, examined by Rabindranath Tagore, Swami Vivekananda and Sri Aurobindo in three separate volumes, can inspire the readers in considering any error, found in the volumes.

Dr Santi Nath Chattopadhyay

'Uttoran': office of ISISAR,
22, S. K. Deb Road (4th bye lane),
Kolkata–700 048. West Bengal, India.
Ph.: 091-33-2521 5753/2534 3782.
Email: cal.isisar@gmail.com
Web: www.isisar.weebly.com

Foreword

The present volume on '**Man, -The Superhuman:** ***A Global Prospect of Expounding Sri Aurobindo's Integral Vision of Humanity'***, written by Dr Santi Nath Chattopadhyay, on the thought and global outlook of Sri Aurobindo represents an important event in the world of humanistic studies. The rich thinking and spirituality of Sri Aurobindo needs to be kept before the consciousness of humankind. For his thought bears directly on our understanding of the future and our human possibilities within that future. As Dr Chattopadhyay shows that Sri Aurobindo's work may be represented in many interconnected ways, a number of insights into our possibilities for a glorious human future. Here, I will mention just three of these insights. *first*, Sri Aurobindo brings us a profound *understanding of religion and spirituality*; *second*, he provides and encompassing *philosophical world view that links the spiritual life* of human beings with emergent evolution; *third*, Sri Aurobindo presents a *powerful humanism,* directed towards our potential humanity.

Regarding the *first insight,* theology, in all the great religious traditions, has often distinguished between beliefs and dogmas, on the one hand, and various forms of spirituality or direct realisation. Spirituality may indeed be coloured and interpreted through religious beliefs, but it needs not be. Some persons throughout history, understood to be highly spiritual, have not professed any religious belief as counterproductive and even harmful to the liberated, spiritual life.

Sri Aurobindo himself understood religion in terms of spirituality. He drew upon the vast Indian religious strategy of Yoga, formulating his own synthesis known as '*integral yoga*', and practiced this discipline throughout his life to actualise within himself ever-more universal levels of spiritual realisation. Religion for Sri Aurobindo arises from, and is empty without, this direct spiritual realisation. This universality of consciousness and love is the heart of religion for Sri Aurobindo. His important philosophy of religion also animates his philosophical worldview, which is a second great contribution emphasised by Dr Chattopadhyay.

The theory of evolution broke into the consciousness of the world most forcefully after the 1859 publication of Darwin's *On the Evolution of Species*. However, thinkers like Sri Aurobindo soon saw that the mechanistic theory advanced by Darwin (random genetic mutations within the context of the natural selection of the fittest to survive) omitted the understanding of evolution as the mysterious ongoing work of God. Such thinkers soon realised that universe, and the integral dimensions of human consciousness, were in the process of an evolution that can be termed "God realisation". God was emerging in and through the process itself and was not simply a *dues ex machine* apart from the process like a watchmaker who sets the clock in motion and has nothing more to do with its operation. This philosophical world view is profoundly developed by Sri Aurobindo in many of his writings. Given our immense spiritual potential for universal consciousness and love, in conjunction with the process of divine emergence within the universe and human history, Sri Aurobindo give us a world view of immense hope and exciting possibilities.

In this background, I develop the present programme as '*Sri Aurobindo and the Paradigm Shift of the 21st Century*'. Sri Aurobindo's integral yoga and theory of the spiritual evolution of humanity provide a substantial contribution to the on-going paradigm shift emerging out of Twentieth Century scientific thought and culminating in the new planetary civilisation of the Twenty-first Century. Sri Aurobindo's life and thought have yet to deeply penetrate the developing philosophy and spirituality of our contemporary world. I am hoping that this book on the thought of Sri Aurobindo contributes toward that end. In this *Foreword*, I will sketch out the frame-work of paradigm transformation characterising the past century and try to show Sri Aurobindo's extra ordinary contribution to this process.

1. The Axial Roots of Our Higher Human Potential

A number of scholars have investigated the great significance of the Axial Period in the history of human civilisation, the period roughly from the eight century to the second century BCE. This period was a period of transformation in the evolutionary development of human consciousness. German Philosopher Karl Jaspers (1953) named this age the Axial Period (Achsenzeit). Great philosophical, ethical and religious teachers arose whose influence resulted in the great religious orientations that continue to dominate the world today.

During the Axial Period, Lao Tzu, Chaung Tzu, and Confucious flourished in China. The *Upanisads* and *Bhagavad Gita* were created in India. Gautama Buddha founded Buddhism in northern India, and Zoroaster taught in Persia. A number of great Hebrew prophets taught in Israel. In Greeklands, the Pre-Socratic philosophers established western philosophy and were followed by the great philosophical visions of Socrates, Plato, Aristotle and Stoicism.

A common human consciousness was emerging worldwide that for the first time was able to distinguish human subjectivity from the objective natural world as well as able to envision the world as a whole in conjunction with an ultimate principle existing behind and above the multiplicity of phenomena. For Lao Tzu and Chaung Tzu, this principle is the Tao. For Confucius, it is the principle of order to which the master of Humanness (jen) conforms his life. For the *Upanishadas* and *Bhagavat Gita,* behind the phenomenal play of existence is the eternal *Brahman*.

In the Mahayana tradition of *Buddhism*, the eternal Buddha nature exists as *dharmakaya*, the unsayable absolute. Zoroaster saw the world as created by Ahura Mazda, the uncreated God. The Hebrew Prophets proclaimed Yahweh as the creator of heaven and earth and redeemer of the people of god. The philosophers of Greece described an unchanging eternal principle that transcended the world and provided the goal and aspiration for human endeavour. Plato termed this the Form of the Good; Aristotle called it the Unmoved Mover; the Stoics referred to it as the cosmic whole or God.

In his classic study-*An Interpretation of Religion: Human Responses to the Transcendent* (2004), philosopher of religion

John Hick understands the emergent consciousness of the Axial Age as projecting human life into an evolutionary mode. A personal subjectivity has now been developed that finds human life to be lacking, infected by sin or ignorance, and feeling the inner demand for salvation or awakening. The missing or lacking element, as understood by all these Axial Period religious teachers and texts, can only be satisfied through a process of conversion from ego-centred consciousness to a consciousness centred on ultimate reality, the ground of being, or God in all these traditions the great teachers and saints have been the ones whose lives have manifested these conversion from ego-centred existence to Reality-centred existence.

One important implication of this interpretation of religion and its emergence within the Axial Period is that the course of individual life as the conversion of consciousness from ego-centredness to Reality-centredness is mirrored in the conversion of human consciousness in general from ego-centricity to supramental consciousness of Reality or God. On the scale of human existence (about two million years), the Axial Period was just yesterday. Since that time, many teachers and mystics have lived who contributed toward humanity's growth. Sri Aurobindo's work provides a crucial twentieth century understanding of this process. However, whereas Hick largely limits the process of God-realisation to our subjective and moral growth in individual human life, Sri Aurobindo sees the conversion from ego-centrism to God-realisation as integral to both individual human life and to cosmic evolution.

In *The Human Cycle*, Sri Aurobindo develops a theory of human evolution that begins with an analysis of the Pre-Axial Vedic Age, which we no longer understand, he says, for we "have lost the mentality" (1970:3). He traces human development through several stages (symbolic, typical, and conventional) to the individualistic and rationalist revolt against conventionalism that finds its realisation in the past several centuries, first in the West, and then in a worldwide influence that "has awakened the slumbering East" (19). The results of this transformation involve the rise of science and, in social theory, the ideals of democracy, human rights, and the right of every person to live a life not predetermined by his or her social role.

However, today we have reached the limits of critical and analytic reason, for these powers cannot illuminate the deeper soul in human beings or the world, and the rationalistic ideal must begin to "subject itself to the ideal of intuitional knowledge and a deeper self-awareness" (24). This new stage in the evolution of human consciousness must end in "the ultimate discovery that man is inwardly a soul and a conscious power of the divine". The discovery of this, and living according to its truth, must ultimately "end by revolutionising his social and collective self-expression"(28).

Two insights emerge from the development of this new "subjectivism". First, that the ego is not the self but rather the soul is a portion of universal Divinity (39) and, Second, that the individual is in solidarity with all humankind, that "we are in our life and being not only ourselves but all others"(40). "It is the practical reorganisation of this truth". Sri Aurobindo writes, "it is the awaking of the soul in man and the attempt to get him to live from his soul and not from his ego which is the inner meaning of religion, and it is that to which the religion of humanity must alive before it can fulfill itself in the life of the race"(1970:547).

Human evolution can move to a manifestation of the true Self, which is greater even than mind. The ideal becomes a progressive transformation of our lives and social existence into embodiments of the transcendent and universal spirit (55). Human evolution is understood by Sri Aurobindo to be a function of the cosmic self-unfolding of the universal Being:

> *The law for humanity is to pursue its upward evolution towards the finding and expression of the Divine in the type of mankind, taking full advantage of the free development and gains of all individuals and nations and grouping of men, to work towards the day when mankind may be reality and not only ideally one divine family, but even then, when it has succeeded in unifying itself, to respect, aid and be aided by the free growth and activity of its individuals and constituent aggregates (64).*

The evolution of human life toward this goal will take planetary civilisation from its present mental age to a spiritual age will mean that there will be a conscious focus on the "essential aim of subjective religions, a new birth, a new consciousness, and upward evolution of the human being" (248). Spiritual evolution will be recognised as our "destiny" and our greatest need. This evolution will be led by people who have become vehicles of the spiritual in every aspect of their being: aesthetic, ethical, mental, and physical. The unity of human life will progressively assimilate the supramental unity of the cosmos and the Divine unity behind all phenomena. "Obscurely", Sri Aurobindo says, "we are now beginning to see something of this behind all our science and philosophy and all our other activities" (230).

2. Holism, Mind, and Evolution in Twentieth Century Science

The amazing growth of science since the seventeenth century, therefore, provides an important aspect of the background necessary for appreciating the work of Sri Aurobindo. The early-modern scientific paradigm that was synthesised by Sir Isaac Newton with the publication of *Principia Mathematica* in 1687 did not yet give us the holism to which Sri Aurobindo refers. Rather, it promoted the competitive individualism and fragmentation that Sri Aurobindo insisted must be superseded by a realisation of holism and unity. Both the system of militarised soverign nation-states and the system of competitive corporate capitalism function as impediments to the further integration and spiritualisation of humanity. For, "the industrial, the commercial, the economic age which is now progressing to its culmination and its close" is "another kind of barbarism" (1970:72).

Classical physics, in particular, failed to discover any place for *mind* within the universe. For Physics understood the cosmos on the model of a machine, constructed from parts (bodies in motion) having only external relations with one another. Mind had no comprehensible place within this paradigm. As contemporary physicist and interpreter of science Henry Stapp puts this: "Classical physics not only fails to demand the mental, it fails to even provide a rational place for the mental. And if the mental is introduced ad hoc, then it must remain totally ineffectual, in absolute contradiction to our deepest experience" (in Kafatos and Nadeau 1999:173).

Two discoveries of twentieth century science going on during Sri Aurobindo's lifetime are especially significant here. The first is the discovery of the holism of the universe and all the phenomena within it. The second is the overcoming of the mind/body separation of early modern science and the emerging recognition that mind is integral to the holism of scientifically observable reality. In their book, *The Conscious Universe: Part and Whole in Modern Physical Theory* (1990), Menas Kafatos and Robert Nadeau make the case, using the latest results of science, that the universe is fundamentally *conscious*. They write:

> *Yet in discovering a new limit to our ability to fully comprehend physical reality, we are presented with a view of nature in which consciousness, or mind, can be properly defined as a phase in the process of the evolution of the cosmos implied in presupposing all other stages. If it manifests or emerges in the later stages, and has been progressively unfolding from the beginning stages, then it world follow that the universe is in some sense conscious (177).*

These thinkers argue that the theoretical paradigms by which we organise our thought impact our "practical reason," that is, our specific ways of organising and acting in human life. They contrast the emerging understanding of holism in the universe (and the senses in which mind appears inseparable from that holism) with the early-modern scientific paradigm that was both materialistic and atomistic:

> *And yet it is also demonstrably true that theoretical reason does over time refashion the terms of construction of human reality within particular linguistic and cultural contexts, and thereby alters the dynamics of practical reason. As many scholars have exhaustively demonstrated, the classical paradigm in physics has greatly influenced and conditioned our understanding and management of human systems of economic and political reality. Virtually all models of this reality treat system as if they consisted of atomized units which interact with one another in terms of laws for forces external to the units. These laws or forces are also assumed to act upon the isolated or isolatable units to form*

hierarchical organisations which are themselves isolated or isotable from other such organisations (181).

The brutal realities of capitalism and political system resting on militarism, power, and domination exist as outmoded artifacts of an early-modern science now superseded by holism–insight into the oneness of humanity and the integral role of mind in the evolutionary process. The paradigm shift that occurred in the twentieth century in biology, social theory, quantum physics and cosmology lays the groundwork for a transformation of human existence, in John Hick's terms, from a fragmented system of militarised nation-states (premised on ego-centred existence) to a holism of unity in diversity (premised on Reality-centred existence).

Darwin's theory of evolution as it was expressed in his book *On the Origin of Species* (1859) drew upon this early-modern paradigm to the extent that it repudiated teleological explanations of evolution in favour of a causal account of random mutations resulting in species variations that were selected out in the struggle for survival among members of various species. However, the discovery of holism in twentieth century science set the stage for an understanding of evolution as *emergent* evolution. Rather than a mechanistic process pushed from behind by random mutations and natural selection evolution began to be understood as the emergence of higher dimensions within the universe through the power of the holism integral to self-organising system and integrated energy fields. As a physicist and interpreter of science Fritjof Capra puts it in his book *The Tao of Physics–An Exploration of the Parallels between Modern Physics and Eastern Mysticism*:

The organising activity of living, self-organising systems, finally, is cognition, or mental activity. This implies a radically new concept of mind, which was first proposed by Gregory Bateson. Mental process is defined as the organising activity of life. This means that all interactions of a living system with its environment are cognitive, or become inseparably connected. Mind, or more accurately, mental process is seen as being immanent in matter at all levels of life. (1975:151)

Mind is no longer seen as an accidental epiphenomenon of the evolutionary process but is now understood to be an integral aspect of the holistic fields within fields discovered by a variety of twentieth century science. Human life, as Sri Aurobindo had understood all along, is no longer a secondary and contingent aspect of the evolutionary process. Humans can now be understood in an entirely different light. Scientist and Roman Catholic Pierre Teilhard de Chardin declares that "the time has come to realise that an interpretation of the universe–even a positivist one–remains unsatisfying unless it covers the interior as well as the exterior of things; mind as well as matter. The true physics is that which will, one day, achieve the inclusion of man in his wholeness in a coherent picture of the world." Man can now be understood "as the axis and leading shoot of evolution" (1959:35-36).

Sri Aurobindo's understanding of the integral relation between human mind and spirituality and the cosmic process appear amazingly prophetic in the light of scientific syntheses that took place after his death in 1950. Henry Stapp describes recent breakthroughs of quantum physics in the following way:

> *The scientific task of explicating this general quantum-mechanical ontology is just beginning. But even the general features of the quantum ontology involve a conception of man and nature profoundly different from the picture provided by classical physics. For man appears no longer as an isolated automaton. He appears rather as an integral part of the highly nonlocal activity of the universe. The revision of the conception of a person, and of his perceived relation to the rest of nature, cannot but have an immense impact on what is perceived as valuable. It must inevitably lead us away from the egocentric bias that was the rational product of the ontology of classical physics, to the values inherent in the image of self, not as a local isolated automaton but rather as a nonlocalizable integrated aspect of the creative impulse of the universe. (1988:57).*

If the human self and the human mind can be thought of, in the light of contemporary scientific breaktroughs, as an "integrated aspect of the creative impulse of the universe," then we are poised once again to consider the thought of Sri Aurobindo. The human mind and human subjectivity become central factors in the gigantic process of cosmic evolution and not merely epiphenomena incidental to a blind materialistic process. Science has revealed a universe in which human beings are an integral part, within which there functions an "anthropic principle" (Harris, 1991) and in which humans are not merely a cosmic accident lost within the vast stellar spaces. Without this understanding, Sri Aurobindo writes, human beings "would be only an insect crawling among other ephemeral insects…amid the appalling immensities of the physical universe" (1973:47).

Human thought and spirituality may now facilitate the process of descent of the divine principle into human life. We are an integral part of an immense cosmic process and our action, or karmayoga, must be to facilitate this process:

> *Life is the first step in the release of consciousness; mind is the second. But the evolution does not finish with mind: it awaits a release into something greater, a consciousness which is spiritual and supramental. The next step of the evolution must be toward the development of Supermind and spirit as the dominant power in the conscious being. For only then will the involved divinity in things release itself entirely and become possible for life to manifest perfection. (1973:29)*

We must take conscious steps to integrate humanity both administratively and spiritually. Sri Aurobindo points out that vast conversions will need to take place in global, social, political, and economic organisation if we are to continue the trajectory of our evolutionary destiny. His vision of human was not merely theoretical, but required practical steps to facilitate the process. He considers these necessary, practical changes in some detail within *The Ideal of Human Unity*.

3. World Union as a Prelude to Spiritual Evolution

We have seen that the proper development of a human being as seen by the great religions involves the overcoming of egoism through the focusing of life on ultimate Reality, according to theologian John

Hick. For Sri Aurobindo, this includes collective egoisms, for example, the overcoming of "huge State egoism" which he characterizes as "brutal, rapacious, cunning, oppressive, intolerant of free action, free speech and opinion, even of freedom of conscience in religion, it preyed upon individuals and classes within as upon weaker nations outside" (1970:281). The real business of a state at the present evolutionary stage of human development is not to act out of collective egoism but to facilitate cooperative action, prevent harmful waste and friction, and remove avoidable injustices (283). But the state apparatus must become universal, a worldwide "parliament of man" (388), encompassing all humanity. We must ascend to "world-union" and become a "federated unity" for all humankind. This is not the spiritual goal, as we have seen, which is the realisation of the Divine within human life. But it has an important function as the next step, laying the groundwork for human spiritual evolution:

> *Such an external or administrative unity may be intended in the near future of mankind in order to accustom the race to the idea of a common life, it its habit, to its possibility; but it cannot be really healthy, durable or beneficial over all the true line of human destiny unless something be developed, more profound, internal and real (284).*

Like his great contemporary, Mahatma Gandhi, Sri Aurobindo cause this functional world–union "a federation of free nations" (329). In 1942, Gandhi introduced a resolution into the Indian National Congress that read "the future peace, security, and order progress of the world demand a world federation of free nations, and on no other basis can the problems of the modern world be solved" (1986:14). In the *ideal of Human Unity,* written long before Gandhi's statement (and published in the journal *Arya* between 1915 and 1918), Sri Aurobindo analyses the possibilities, dangers, and features of developing such a federation at great length. But once begun, he says, whatever difficulties and setbacks were encountered, "it will be impossible for mankind to drawback" and whatever trials had to be endured "would be bound to help in the end rather than hinder the final and inevitable result" (365).

The fundamental principle of the federation of free nations will be neither a totalitarian uniformity nor an anarchic diversity but the principle of unity in diversity:

> *But freedom is as necessary to life as law and regime; diversity is as necessary as unity to our true completeness... At the same time, while diversity is essential for power and fruitfulness of life, unity is necessary for its order, arrangement and stability. Unity we must create, but not necessarily uniformity. If man could realise a perfect spiritual unity, no sort of uniformity would be necessary; for the utmost play of diversity would be securely possible on that foundation (401).*

We need, he says, "a world-union founded upon the principle of liberty and variation in a free and intelligent unity" (422). "The unity of the human race to be entirely sound in consonance with the deepest laws of life must be founded on free groupings, and the groupings again must be the natural association of free individuals" (490-91).

Sri Aurobindo died in 1950, leaving his spiritual partner the Mother (Mira Rischard) in charge of the continued development of his vision and the movement that had developed around his powerful teachings. He wrote that he had no doubt about the depth of realisation of the Mother and her capacity to further bring the Divine realisation to the earth:

> *There is one divine force which acts in the universe and in the individual and is also beyond the individual and the universe. The Mother stands for all these, but she is working here in the body to bring down something not yet expressed in this material world so as to transform life here–it is so that you should regard her as the divine Shakti working here for that purpose. She is that in the body, but in her whole consciousness she is also indentified with all the other aspects of the Divine (1973, 20-21).*

In 1958, World Union was created under the direction of the Mother as an international organisation working for the global unification in *The Ideal of Human Unity.* That same year, the World Constitution and Parliament Association (WCPA) was founded in the United States by Philip Isely and others with the purpose of writing a *Constitution for the Federation of Earth* (Martin, 2010). There was immediate mutual recognition between the two organisations.

During the three decades following 1970, Samar Basu and A.B. Patel, both major leaders in World Union, also served as leaders within the World Constitution and Parliament Association. A.B. Patel was General Secretary and Treasurer of World Union International Centre, Sri Aurobindo Ashram, Pondicherry. Like Basu, he participated in the first three Constitution Assemblies in 1968, 1977 and 1979 during which world citizens from many countries worked together to envision, write, and promote the *Earth Constitution* to all the governments of Earth. Patel presided over the signing of the initial version of the *Earth Constitution* at the Constituent Assembly in Innsbruck, Austria in 1977 and was its very first signatory. From this time until his death; he was Co-President of WCPA with Dr Reinhart Ruge of Mexico. He was also elected as Parliamentary Speaker for the first session of the Provisional World Parliament held under the authority of the *Constitution* that took place in Brighton, England in 1982.

Samar Basu was a noted Bengali author who first visited Pondicherry in 1967, joining World Union in 1973. He soon became Editor of *World Union Journal* and lectured widely on Sri Aurobindo's philosophy. Basu was also a signatory to the *Earth Constitution* during the Second Assembly. His book, *The UNO, The World Government and the Ideal of World Union as Envisioned by Sri Aurobindo* chronicles many of these events. Dr Terence Amerasinghe of Sri Lanka, as Co-President of the World Constitution and Parliament Association after Patel's death, wrote the Preface for this 1999 book in which Amerasinghe quotes from the Mother's Message to the Peoples of the World at the Birth Centenary of Sri Aurobindo in 1972: "A new world based on Truth and refusing the old slavery of falsehood, wants to take birth. In all countries there are people who know it, at least feel it. To them we call, will you collaborate?" (iv-v). Basu saw the connection between World Union and WCPA in an almost mystical light. In this book, he writes:

> *...The World Union as an international organisation was set up in 1958 under the direct guidance of the Mother (of Sri Aurobindo*

Ashram, Pondicherry), to work for Human Unity and World Peace and harmony on spiritual foundation by Sri Aurobindo and that WCPA was also founded in 1958 as an international organisation to achieve the same goal in its own way. The formation of these two organisations in the same has a deep occult significance which has yet to be realised (58-59).

For many years Amerasinghe was Co-president of the World Constitution and Parliament Association with Dr Reinhart Ruge from Mexico. Both were regular visitors to Pondicherry and Auroville and collaborators with World Union in the work for democratic world government under the *Constitution for the Federation of Earth.* Amerasinghe and Ruge recognised the significance of the work of Sri Aurobindo and the Mother and made the evident connections between the *Earth Constitution* and Sri Aurobindo's great vision of the evolution of human life toward "Supermind", toward ever-greater unification and spiritual realisation.

Ruge and Patel had met in Delhi in 1975. Patel immediately invited Ruge to Pondicherry, after which time they become good friends. Ruge retired in 2003 to become WCPA Honorary President for Life and Amerasinghe continued as WCPA President until his death at age 90 in 2007. Both Ruge and Amerasinghe understood human life through the model of the emergence of higher level of human existence, one major step for which would be the ratification of the *Constitution for the Federation of Earth.* Each of them understood that "the ascent to the Divine Life is the human journey, the Work of works, the acceptable sacrifice. This alone is man's real business in the world and the justification of his existence...(1973:46-47)". Perhaps this is why these leaders spent so much time in India. India is not only a centre of the great insight into the human ascent to the Divine, but its multiple wisdom traditions lend themselves to an understanding of the need for the dynamic unity in diversity envisioned by the Preamble to the *Earth Constitution:* "the principle of unity in diversity is the basis for a new age when war shall be outlawed and peace prevail; when the earth's total resources shall be equitably used for human welfare; and when basic human rights and responsibilities shall be shared by all without discrimination" (Martin, 2010:28). In the profound word of Sri Aurobindo, "the universe and the individual are necessary to each other in their ascent" (1973:49).

The praxis of these activists on behalf of the *Earth Constitution* recalls the Karmayoga of Mahatma Gandhi and Sri Aurobindo. Sri Aurobindo writes: "The soul in us develops itself by life and works, and indeed not so much as the action itself but the way of our soul's inner force of working determines its inner relations to Spirit. This is, indeed, the justification of Karmayoga as a justification of the soul's higher self-realisation" (117). The praxis of organisation on behalf of World Union must necessarily be complemented by the praxis of Integral Yoga as developed by Sri Aurobindo.

In their discourse on Education, Sri Aurobindo and the Mother affirm that *collective reorganisation* for humanity is just as fundamental as individual self-realisation: "In this effort, however, to improve human conditions there have always been two tendencies, which although apparently contrary to each other should rather be complementary and together work of the progress. One seeks a collective reorganisation, something that would toward an effective unity of mankind: the other that all progress is made first by the individual who should be given the conditions in which he can progress freely. Both are equally true and necessary, and our effort should be directed along both lines. Collective progress and individual progress are interdependent" (227).

The history of WCPA remains linked to Sri Aurobindo and World Union. Despite the appearances today of seemingly insurmountable obstacles to actively promote the *Earth Constitution* with ever- growing recognition. We share a common understanding that next step for human beings can and must be political and constitutional union under the *Earth Constitution*. It alone will make possible the further descent of the Divine into human life.

Sri Aurobindo practiced spiritual discipline for many years, from his first realisation upon reading the *Gita* as a young man in the Alipore prison (1973:7-8) to his development of the "*Integral Yoga*" system of his mature years as "his programme for historical transformation gained a universal expression essential for contemporary religious thought" (9). He realised that transformation of consciousness and the descent of the Divine within himself was nothing unique but simply an actualisation of a universal spiritual capacity belonging to all human beings. And he understood that his own spiritual realisation pointed to a process that was fundamental to history and humanity.

He showed in his life and work that, through Divine grace, humans could undertake a conscious evolution that would elevate human life beyond man to Superman as Superhuman, beyond egoistic to the Life Divine. He understood his own realisation of higher consciousness "not as a coincidence or fortuitous accident, but as a sanction as a sanction and seal of the Divine Power" (1973:11). At the age of seventy five, he wrote of the meaning of India's role in world affairs and of his life's work as the articulation of "a new step in the evolution which, by uplifting the consciousness to a higher level , would begin the solution of many problems of existence which have perplexed and vexed humanity, since men began to think and to dream of individual perfection and a perfect society"(11). Here lies Sri Aurobindo's profound contribution to the transformation of the twenty first century.

The breakthroughs in contemporary science, the process of ratifying the *Earth Constitution,* and the immense contribution of Sri Aurobindo, together lay the groundwork for the propound paradigm shift characterising our present century. Science has discovered the key role of human beings in cosmic evolution, and the movement for human unity understands that we must convert our lives from ego-centric existence to fullness of Reality, which Sri Aurobindo spiritually experienced as an ever-fuller of the Divine within our lives. I am quite sure that this impressive volume on Sri Aurobindo will make a significant contribution to this process of inspiring a deep paradigm shift. With Sri Aurobindo, we understand that a great evolutionary movement is in progress, one that can fundamentally transform human life at any time: "if earth calls and the Supreme answers, the hour can be even for that immense and glorious transformation" (57).

For '...immense and glorious transformation' Sri Aurobindo observed a great evolutionary movement in progress where WCPA

Projects his philosophy of 'World Union' in organising 'Federation of Earth Movement' for the introduction of 'Earth Constitution' with the development of 'Federal World Parliament' and 'Federal World Government'. This process of evolution, according to Dr Chattapadhyay, is intercultural. He, in the light of Sri Aurobindo, organises 'Intercultural World Peace Movement' at the grass root level of society which is purely non-violent and evolutionary process of 'intercommunication' of ideas and ideals, present in each individual, culture and community, in developing 'intercultural relation and understanding' with an advancement of essential process of 'Culture', as 'Cultivation' of human values in evolving global value as 'Universal Good'.

In this background, the 'Intercultural World Peace Movement', organised by Dr Chattopadhyay through his society–ISISAR (International Society for Intercultural Studies and Research), is closely associated with 'Federation of Earth Movement' which reflects Sri Aurobindo's idea of human unity and it is purely non-violent, evolutionary and spiritual; as a prospect of developing glorious future of mankind as 'World Union'.

In this humanistic process of evolution of mankind, a third powerful theme rightly articulated by Dr Chattopadhyay is Sri Aurobindo's *humanism*. The debate over *humanism* rages to this day among both religious people and those who claim to be non-religious. Among the religious people the central issue appears to be whether God manifests such glory and power independently of human beings that man is diminished to the point where his role is and should be only a self deprecating humility. Are human beings merely a sinful nothing in relation to God, utterly dependent on gratuitous grace for their redemption? Religious *humanism*, and the humanism of Sri Aurobindo says 'no'. Human beings are called to responsibility and creativity in relation to God. Human beings, indeed, must be open to God through a holistic karma yoga in which action, meditation, and everyday existence combine to allow the Divine descent into our lives and the life of our species. Our responsibility and creativity are essential to this process, and in this sense, the future is significantly up to us.

It is here that Dr Chattopadhyay rightly emphasises the theme of the Superman as Superhuman. In the West, this word retains a certain negative connotation due to its development by Nietzsche as a response to nihilism. Nietzsche's celebration of 'hardness' and a 'festival of cruelty' in the service of creating a superior human beings capable of 'creating values' in the face of the valuelessness of existence must also be seen in the light of its abuse and perversion by the Nazis who perpetuated the myth of the superior, compassionless 'blonde beast'. It is important, therefore, that Sri Aurobindo's use of the word '*Superman*' as Superhuman being has been emphasised in this book. Our Human destiny, that which will turn our 'human all–too human' weakness into 'super-humanity', will be the actualisation of universal love and compassion in which the unity of the human family will be affirmed inseparably from its wonderful diversity, with no one, no race, religion, or culture excluded. The *humanism* of Sri Aurobindo is an all embracing *humanism* not only with respect to its universality but also with respect to the responsibility that it places upon human beings. This is a third theme that Dr Chattopadhyay illuminates in detail. In these several ways, Dr Chattopadhyay has given us this very important book on Sri Aurobindo as his own gift to humanity.

Dr Glen T. Martin,
Professor of Philosophy,
Religion and Peace Studies,
Radford University, USA.
President, WCPA & IPPNO, USA,
Chief Patron, ISISAR, India

Works Cited

Aurobindo, Sri (1970), *The Human Cycle, The ideal of Human Unity*. War and Self-Determination, Sri Aurobindo Ashram, Pondicherry, India.

Aurobindo Sri (1972), *Collected Writings in Twenty-two Volumes*. Sri Aurobindo Ashram, Pondicherry, India.

Aurobindo Sri (1973), The Essential Aurobindo, Robert McDermott, ed, Schocken Books, New York, USA.

Basu, Samar (1999), *The UNO, the World Government and the ideal of World Union*, World Union Publisher, Pondicherry, India.

Capra, Fritjot (1975), *The Tao of Physics-An Exploration of the Parallels Between Modern Physics and Eastern Mysticism,* Shambhala, Berkeley, USA.

Chattopadhyay, Santi Nath (1987), *The Universal Man,* Naya Prokash, Kolkata, India.

Chattopadhyay, Santi Nath Ed (2005), *The World Peace*, Punthipustak, Kolkata, India.

Chattopadhyay, Santi Nath Ed (2010), *Violence and Non-violence: A Global Perspective*, Punthipustak, Kolkata, India.

Gandhi, Mahatma (1986), *Quoted in Tom A. Hudgens, Late's Abolish War*, Denva: BILR Corporation Harris, Errol E (1991), *A Cosmos and Anthropos.* A Philosophical Interpretation of the Anthropic Cosmological Principle, London: Humanities Press International.

Hick, John (2004), *An Interpretation of Religion:Human Responses to the transcendent.* Second edition. New Haven: Yale University Press.

Jaspers, Karl (1953), *The Origin and Goal of History.* New Haven: Yale University Press.

Kafatos, Menas and Nadeau, Robert (1990), *The Concious Universe: Part and Whole in Modern Physical Theory.* Berlin: Springer–Verlag.

Martin, Glen T (2010), *Constitution for the Federation of Earth* With Historical *Introduction, Commentary and Conclusion.* Pamplin, VA: Institute or Economic Democracy Press.

Teilhard De Chardin, Pierre (1959), *The Phenomenon of Man.* Bernard Wall, trans. New York: Harper and Brothers.

Stapp, Henry (1988), *"Quantum Theory and the Physicist's Conception of Nature: Philosophical Implication of Bell's Theoren".* In Richard F. Kiechener, ed. The World View of Contemporary physics: Does it Need a New Metaphysics? Albeny, State University of New York Press.

INTRODUCTION: *MAN, The Superhuman:* Sri Aurobindo's Integral Vision of the Religion of Humanity

The present work examines the philosophical and religious experiences of Sri Aurobindo from a humanist perspective which is also present in the philosophy of religion of the contemporary Indian thinkers like Swami Vivekananda, Rabindranath, Mahatma Gandhi, S. Radhakrishnan and others. The work is expository, comparative and critical in a form of modern evaluation from East-West perspectives.

Religion occupies an important position in human life and society. In different forms and symbols it exists and functions in every society of the world. Different human needs and desires like growth, existence, self-development etc. and faith in a supreme or superhuman power on whom a man can depend for his well-being are reflected in religion and it involves different ritualistic procedure, for the achievement of the favour of supreme power which is manifested through different human activities in a social and institutional form. So the study of man and human society becomes incomplete if it does not include the study of religion and philosophy. If a comprehensive survey of the human experience and society is made, it will be found that from the earliest times and throughout the ages, religion is intimately related with human life that reveals a complete view about the history of man. For this, Comte, a positivist, recognises that religion contains the whole of human existence. Max Muller also repeats the same opinion that the true history of man is the history of religion. But be it noted they cherish a specific view of religion, but Sri Aurobindo, we shall see, introduces a comprehensiveness in religious consciousness, not found in them.

Indian Spiritualism, is not divorced from the human life and existence. It centres round the idea of religion as the Hindu view of life which is the establishment of spiritual brotherhood among men through the eternal bond of love. If the inner spirit of the Contemporary Indian Philosophy is carefully examined, we may find the similar idea of religion as the spiritual development of human life and existence, expressing eternal and intimate relation with all, which, according to Dr Radhakrishnan, is a 'spiritual fellowship'. The development of this 'spiritual fellowship' as the inter-relation among men in the world is the fundamental object of the Indian outlook of religion, presented in *Hinduism,* which has its roots in *Vedas*, *Upanishads* and other systems of Indian Philosophy and can also be revealed in different thoughts and activities of different contemporary Indian thinkers. Dr A.C. Das thus observes, "If one wants to get to the core of Hinduism as a religion, one must understand the theistic movement which has its roots...........in the *Vedas* and *Upanishads,* and has had its periodic fruitions, chief among the latest being Sri Ramakrishna, Swami Vivekananda, Mahatma Gandhi, Sri Aurobindo and Rabindranath."[1]

Among these thinkers, only the religious ideas of Sri Aurobindo are to be critically evaluated with reference to religious ideas of his contemporaries due to some similarities and differences among these thinkers. But it should be noted in this connection, that inspite of similarities and inter-relations of thoughts, there are several differences among them. Still it must be pointed out that inspite of several differences, the religious views of these thinkers, centre round the idea of man and the development of human life and existence, according to them, should be the fundamental procedure of religion. This human outlook of religion, inspires these thinkers to open their hearts and feelings for the interpretations of *Vedas*, *Upanishads* and other traditional Indian views of life that compel them to establish religious institutions or *Ashramas* i.e. *Santiniketan* by *Rabindranath*, *Ramakrishna Mission*, by Vivekananda and *Sri Aurobindo Ashramas* at Pondicherry, by Sri Aurobindo, only to preach the humanitarian views of religion, expressing the eternal ideal of unity or interrelation among men in this world. These institutional procedures of religion, introduced by these thinkers, do not follow any rigid religious principle that can suppress the potentiality in man, but these can try to emancipate religion from superstitions, orthodoxy, idolatry and other limitations and contradictions of human life. So religion, according to these thinkers, is not the imposition of any rigid principle or dogma on man, but it, on the other hand, it is the natural or eternal expression of human nature, manifesting potential perfection in man. The manifestation of perfection in man, is the development of his religious consciousness which is the realisation of the highest human value or divinity, manifested in the final state of accomplishment as the freedom in unity, expressing the universality in the human existence that fundamentally makes religion as the religion of Man, the Universal or Infinite as Superhuman. This is nothing but the eternal and the essential expression of potential universality or infiniteness in the human existence.

For the development of this state of universality or infiniteness in the highest state of human freedom, developing unity or interrelation among men in this world, Rabindranath prescribes the human procedure that is the realisation of love through the selfless service of mankind which develops the spirit of universality as Absolute Love or Bliss in human existence, expressing the idea of the divinity of man. In this context of developing the spirit of universality, Vivekananda prefers the supramoral procedure or *Yogas* for the development of power as Absolute in love with power, developing spiritual brotherhood among men. Sri Aurobindo, on the other hand, introduces the supramental method of *Yoga* or divine union for the realisation of spiritual unity through the transformation of individual and collective states of existence as the synthesis of materiality, sociality and spirituality for the introduction of divinity in man and society. But, however, through these different methods they ultimately try to develop the integral and human outlook of religion that is an establishment of unity or harmony among men in this world. The present work deals with Sri Aurobindo's idea of religion that represents his integral and human outlook. Religion, according to him, centres round the idea of man that stands on the evolution of human nature, towards the eternal manifestation of his potential perfection in the realisation of freedom, -developing unity and introducing divinity in human life and society. In this context, religion is not taken as the imposition of something on man, but it is the essential expression of human nature itself. Man, on the other hand, also stands on religion which finally expresses his potential universality. He thus finally develops the nature of religion as a Universal phenomenon. So, religion, in this sense, is man's universal nature, that, according to Sri Aurobindo, is the expansion of the *Superhuman* in human process and existence. This essential and harmonious development of human nature and existence, in the insightful observation of Sri Aurobindo, finally leads to the introduction of divine unity in the individual and social existences of man that is the development of The 'Life Divine' on earth.

This work on Sri Aurobindo, is divided into four chapters. *The First Chapter* on *The Background of Sri Aurobindo's Philosophy of Religion of Man, The Superhuman: An Evolutionary Progress of Integral Human Outlook* with *Part-i.* on *Impact of Education and Social Trainings; Part-ii.* on *Importance of The Integral Idea of Revolutionary Nationalism in the Freedom of Man and Mother-land* and *Part-iii.* on *Significance of Integral View in developing Unity in Man and Society* are to deal with the background of the development of Sri Aurobindo's Idea of the Religion as essentially related to Man's evolutionary progress of life and thought, representing Sri Aurobindo's *universal* outlook in expanding integral process of human existence.

The Second Chapter on *the Meaning and the Nature of the Philosophy of Religion: An Integral Development of Divinity in Man and World*, with *Part-i.* on *The Religion and Religionism; Part-ii.* on *Importance of the Integral View of Sri Aurobindo in cultivating Religion as the Realisation of Man, The Superhuman* and *Part-iii.* on *The Divine Life on Earth and the ways of attaining the state of Human Freedom.* All these parts under chapter two discuss the meaning, the nature and significance of the Integral Outlook in developing Religion, as Religion of Man, The *Superhuman*.

This idea of the religion as associated with Nature, is harmonious expression of the potential universality in man that finally *leads* him to develop the divine unity in individual and social states and processes.

The Third Chapter on *Sri Aurobindo's Religion of Man, The Superhuman: A Critical and Comparative Evaluation* with *part-i.* on *Examination of the ideas and ways of developing Man, The Superhuman,* and *part-ii.* on *An Integral Development of the Theory of Creative Man and the Philosophy of Humanism.*

The Fourth Chapter on Concluding Observations: A Global Prospect of Expounding Sri Aurobind's Integral Vision of Humanity, deals with the concluding estimates of the entire discussions on the humanistic study of Sri Aurobindo's Philosophy of Religion as an integral development of the nature and existence of Man as *Superhuman.* The proposed work intends to give us a critical and comparative estimates of the idea of religion, present in contemporary Indian philosophy. The object of this work is to deal with the humanistic approach to the Philosophy of Religion of Sri Aurobindo, developing The Theory of Creative Man or *Sristisheel Manavbad.* I have collected the views of Sri Aurobindo from his numerous Bengali and English writings. So far as the Bengali works are concerned I have either quoted from authentic translations or I myself have translated the passages into English. I have taken utmost precaution in doing the translations; still if I have misrepresented any idea, the fault is entirely mine. Before I close, I express my deep and sincere gratitude to the distinguished Indian and Western Thinkers and Scholars whose works or public lectures or valuable suggestions were of great help to me. In this context, I express my gratefulness to Dr Glen T Martin, Radford University, USA for writing a stimulating Foreword on this theme. In the preparation of this work I also acknowledge the different types of assistance from my publisher and members of ISISAR for in making this venture a reality.

Chapter - 1

The Background of Sri Aurobindo's Philosophy of Religion of Man, The Superhuman: An Evolutionary Progress of Integral Human Outlook

Part - I

Impact of Education and Social Trainings

Religion as *Dharma* is the primary basis of Indian way of life that influences the Social, Cultural, Political, Educational and Moral outlook of the Indians and thus it occupies an important position in the systematic development of Indian philosophy that finally leads to the inauguration of *religious Humanism* in the socio-cultural and socio-political thoughts of contemporary Indian thinkers. Different contemporary Indian thinkers like Sri Ramkrishna, Swami Vivekananda, Rabindranath Tagore and others have tried to explain the social existence of man that expresses his religious nature as the essential part of human life. Sri Aurobindo, like all these thinkers, evaluates the different aspects of human life that reveal the religious existence of man in a systematic form on the basis of the synthesis of philosophical and religious outlook of human life. This integral or integral development of the life of man, in the opinion of Sri Aurobindo, is the evaluation of human life towards completeness that expresses the essential nature or divine existence of man as the Religion of Man.

The development of human life towards the completeness in and through the material orders of life, according to Rabindranath Tagore, is dependent on the '*meditation on humanity*', which to Sri Aurobindo, is the expression of '*divinity*' in man that reveals his essential nature or religion of life as harmony. This Integral outlook of Sri Aurobindo, includes man in religious milieu and places religion on man as the essential part of his evolutionary process. Thus, the religious life of man from Sri Aurobindo's insightful perspective-is the integral development of human life in a process of evolution towards a unity in man, transcending the contradictions of his material existence. This urges him continuously from within, to sacrifice his poor or individual interests in a pursuit of love and service of mankind, for establishing peace and harmony in society.

In order to understand the significance of this integral process of Sri Aurobindo's Religion of Man and its essential and eternal relation with human life–we have to go through the evolutionary progress and integral development of Sri Aurobindo's thought and life in different stages under the influence of different humanitarian views which may be taken as the background of his religious philosophy. The evolutionary progress of Sri Aurobindo's thought and life, demonstrates that though man exists in the milieu of varied contradictions of material world,–still he can overcome these contradictions, through a gradual manifestation of the superior orders of human outlook as an integral process potentially present in him. The expression of this potential nature of man is to manifest the integrality of his existence as an element between his individuality and social process involved in life. This ideal of an inner unity and integrality in the human existence is progressively developed and manifested in the different stages of individual and social life. It may be evaluated differently in the background of man's evolutionary process through social process in its transformed lift towards a mystic or spiritual order which Sri Aurobindo realised through his life. This is explained by Dr Rao thus: "His mystical experience has revealed to him the secrets of human existence, the significance of human life and the goal of man."[1]

So, for the evaluation of man is a realisation of religion and philosophy in human–social situation. This, according to Aurobindo, is necessary to recount the factors that build up his humanitarian view, developed through his life–history, which has a reference to his early and a continuous progress of his family, and social life with later transformations leading to his final choice for an *Ashramic* life at Pondicherry. These were the concrete forum of his voluminous writings in English, both in prose and poetry, outmoding or even challenging the literary achievements of England and Europe as a whole, reflecting the mastery of his efficiency in Western Classics, while as a student in England and after his return to India, -his similar efficiency in Indian Classics.

Importance of the National and the Humanitarian View, Present in the Early Family Life

Sri Aurobindo's Idea of the religion of Man refers to his life and heritage as the background of his thought that was very much influenced by the humanitarian view; developed in his family life. In this connection it may be said that the life of Sri Aurobindo was very much important in history as it was a historical necessity which was also a continuous exercise in perfection and transformation of life to progressive higher orders-by literary expressions. His life and message through his writings–are for helping a man to realise his own perfection through a transcendence of the material, political and social orders, of a spirit seeking a freedom from the lower orders, not by ignoring them, but perfecting them, through one's progressive higher Nature.

In the progress of Sri Aurobindo's human outlook, the Influence of India's spiritual, cultural and social factors, as reflected in his family life have to be considered in the true spirit of India's cultural heritage from the *Vedas* and the *Upanishads*, with a progress beyond later *Vedantic* and *Yogic* ideas and practices. In the 15th August of 1872, he was born in the family of his parents Dr Krishnadhan Ghosh and Swarnalata, at the house of a Barrister Manmohan Ghosh, at Theatre Road in Calcutta, under British rule of Exploitations. Sri Aurobindo's father Dr Krishnadhan was a friend of Manmohan who was a lover of motherland and went to England at the direction of first Congress President Umesh Banerjee for the presentation of the aims and objects of Indian National Congress. Dr Ghosh was the eldest son-in-law of Acharya Rajnarayan Basu, the educationist, social and religious reformer and was credited with an honour of a "Grand Father of Indian Nationalism". His humanitarian views developed through his thoughts and activities, presented a true picture of an Indian way of life in love with the scientific view of the West that influenced his grandson

Sri Aurobindo in the development of his integral human outlook. Accepting these eternal spirit of integrality–Sri Aurobindo, in connection with the death of Rajnarayan, -wrote in his sonnet: "Not in annihilation lost, nor given

> To darkness art thou fled from us and light,
> O strong and sentient spirit;..........."[2]

It may be observed thus that the social environment of Barrister Ghosh's house where Sri Aurobindo was born, and the enlightened qualities of his parents and grandfather–influenced him very much. He also was influenced by his mother Swarnalata, -an educated, religious and devotional lady and father Krishnadhan Ghosh, about whom Sri Aurobindo wrote with a deep feeling: ".........sharp–intelligent, soft-hearted, emotional, recklessly charitable, indifferent to own want, but excited for other's sorrows and sufferings......."[3]

So the compassionate and enlightened attributes of his parents and inspiring qualities of his youngest brother Barindra Kumar–a nationalist, freedom fighter and a great revolutionary, -made him a real thinker about man and motherland. Regarding the evaluation of this influence of the humanitarian views, present in his family, in the context of traditional Indian spirit, it may be pointed out, -"Under the influence of the eternal sacrificial ideal of India, the centre of human love, through the influence of different human qualities of Rajnarayan Basu, the great *Acharya of Nationalism,* and his parents, the beloved persons of the great *Acharya* and with a close contact with the youngest brother Barindra Kumar, a devoted freedom fighter, Sri Aurobindo became a real priest of the hymns of man's freedom."[4]

Impact of Education and Social Trainings

The Humanitarian spirit of Sri Aurobindo, emerging out of the traditional and social outlook, became articulate through his writings, reflecting his special educations in England and letter study of the Indian Classics since the *Vedas*. This training of Sri Aurobindo started with the integral vision of both the west and the east, particularly India which he modernised in the background of the scientific analysis of European Education. In this connection it may be noted thus: "Aurobindo's father Dr Krishnadhan, -true to his own deep convictions and inconformity with the practice of many other educated Indians of his time who had capitulated to the glamour of the West-wished to give his children a wholly European type of education".[5] At the age of five years, Aurobindo, along with his two brothers, were sent to Loreto Convent School at Darjeeling which was for the training of the children of European Officials. But we can know a little information about the period of two years (1877–79) of Aurobindo's school life. However in 1879, Aurobindo was taken by his father to England, where he was under the private training of Mr and Mrs Drewett and under the influence of the western culture at Drewett's family, in Manchester from 1879 to September 1884 when he learned Latin. From September 1884 to July 1890, he was under the training of St. Paul's School in London where he learned Greek. From October 1890 to October 1892, he was at Cambridge under King's College with a Senior Classical Scholarship of £80 per year and proved his efficiency before Oscar Browning, the man of eminence in Cambridge. He, in this period paid more attention to reading and writing English poetry and in the serious study of English, French and other classical literature, History, etc. This European education and training thus "seems to have been the most formative in his cultural make-up and intellectual equipment",[6] during the formative period of his life-which made him self-conscious about the free existence of man in his material and social life.

In 1890, Aurobindo passed Indian Civil Service Examination, but he deliberately ignored the importance of appearing in riding examination because he did not want to serve under the British rule of India and he gave priority to foster the sense of human existence in freedom. This realisation of the sense of freedom both in material and social life, -urged Aurobindo to become the active member of '*Indian Majlis*', where he expressed his revolutionary attitude about the need of the freedom of India.

This broad humanistic attitude of Aurobindo undoubtedly emerged out of his understanding the best of both Western and Indian cultural processes of his time. During the period of his life in Cambridge-he concentrated on his studies for the Tripos and ICS Examinations, but for self-improvement, he participated in the activities of the

Majlis-and for deriving some inspiration, he cultivated writing poetry for developing insightful vision. Sri Purani explained this in the following way: "The chief preoccupations of Aurobindo at Cambridge were, 1. Studies for the Tripos and the I.C.S. 2. Participation in the Indian Majlis, and zeal for Indian Independence. 3. Writing Poetry."[7] A careful examination of these sides of Aurobindo's life in England proves that the influence of European education on him made him a master of different languages like Greek, Latin, English, French, Italian, German, etc., that these finally helped him to enter into the intrinsic nature of European culture. The development of the cultural pursuits, refined his inner self, so that he could be gradually detached from his narrow self-interests, and materialist proneness.

He demonstrated his intellectual efficiency through his success in obtaining the Tripos and the necessary credits in ICS Examination, but his main interest was riveted to his idea of human freedom. This thinking in Aurobindo finally made him conscious about the freedom of his own country and countrymen that inspired him to participate in the discussions about the liberation of India in *'Indian Majlis'*. Regarding this participation, it was observed that "His attention was now drawn to India and this feeling was soon canalised into the idea of the liberation of his own country. But the "firm decision" took full shape only towards the end of another four years. It has already been made when he went to Cambridge and as a member and for sometime secretary of the *Indian Majlis* at Cambridge he delivered many revolutionary speeches which, as he afterwards learnt, had their part in determining the authorities to exclude him from the Indian Civil Service; the failure in the riding test was only the occasion, for in some other cases an opportunity was given for remedying this defect in India itself."[8]

Thus, it may be observed that his feeling for freedom of his own country and countrymen, revealed through his thoughts and activities in England, finally created a feeling of love for humanity as a whole-as expressed through his poetic emotion. This poetic spirit of Aurobindo was revealed through many of his English poems that finally became manifest in a supramental integral mode of his thought and cultural outlook about man as the eternal being, in and through life's contradictions. This view of Aurobindo was expressed in his poetry very aptly thus:

> "Love, a moment drop thy hands
> Night within my soul expands.
> Veil thy beauties milk-rose-fair
> In that dark and showering hair.
> Coral kisses ravish not
> When the soul is tinged with thought"[9]

The eternal unity in human existence is possible only, 'when the soul is tinged with thought', and this unity according to Aurobindo, becomes complete in love. This poetic spirit of Aurobindo gradually developed a human outlook that inspired him to think about others, rather than to think about his own restricted self or ego. He, thus started thinking about his poor and undeveloped country where he was born and about his exploited countrymen who were his brothers and sisters. He was no more satisfied with his mere acquisition of knowledge through English education and training. This feeling for his country and his countrymen helped him to develop his keen sense of nationalism, and stimulated his flare for social service that required another kind of training to be obtained from Indian cultural processes. To realise the comparative broad vision of an intercultural process, he started for Baroda and joined Baroda service on 8th February, 1893 and spent thirteen years from 1893 to 1906. He started his service in the Settlement Department, then served in the Stamps and Revenue Departments and finally joined Baroda College as part-time lecturer of French, then became the Professor of English and lastly the Vice-Principal. In this period of life, he came in contact with several persons like Maharaja of Baroda, Lieutenant Madhavrao Jadhav and through their influences, he was engaged in different social and educational works. But the significance of all these activities, lies in the development of his inner human outlook about progressive freedom from the restricted processes of the material, the social, and the mental levels of one's psyche. His was an attempt to rise to the transcendent levels of one's supra-mental processes, which led him to inquire into the cultural processes of India, in the milieu of which he was born, and influenced by some persons of his own family.

This view of human freedom as glimpsed by Aurobindo during this period of his life in India after his return from England, was advanced under the joint influence of European or scientific education and culture and the traditional, eternal and spiritual way of Indian life. The contradictions which he confronted between the materialist and spiritualist outlook of two great traditions of the West and the East, Aurobindo's thought could be resolved from a broader perspective towards life. His was a suggestion for spiritual lift of man. Regarding the first experience of this nature, Aurobindo wrote, "Since I set foot on the Indian soil on the Apollo Bunder in Bombay, I began to have spiritual experiences, but these were not divorced from this world but had an inner and infinite bearing on it, such as a feeling of the Infinite pervading material space and immanent inhabiting material objects and bodies. At the same time I found myself entering superphysical world and planes with influences and an effect from them upon the material plane".[10] This realisation of the new significance of material existence, in the background of a transcendent infinite process, transformed Aurobindo's mind totally. His was no longer an inspiration from any abstract thought or philosophy and metaphysics of the West. He became inclined to search for the spiritual recesses of Indian thought, the materials of which he discerned from his studies and teachings of Sri Ramkrishna and from the writings of Swami Vivekananda. The concrete human and integral outlook as brought out by Swami Vivekananda influenced Aurobindo to think about man in a very special yet in a natural manner.

Social Significance of Marriage and Married Life

The natural development of Aurobindo's human outlook could be found in his expressed desire to enter into the married life. Expressing this desire, he published an advertisement in the newspaper which arrested the attention of Sri Girish Chandra Bose, the renowned educationist and the founder of Bangabasi College, an Institution of National Importance, at Calcutta, in organising education for the people of Bengal and by the sons of the soil of Bengal against Government Colleges and Missionary Colleges under Foreign Control. This movement of National Education was guided by Pandit Ishwar Chandra Vidyasagar and expanded by Girish Chandra and others, and the spirit of National Education was expanded by Aurobindo in an effective manner. Regarding the marriage of Aurobindo, Girish Chandra took active interest in developing the married life of Aurobindo with Mrinalini Devi, the daughter of Sri Bhupal Bose, an intimate friend of Girish Chandra. On 16th Baisakh of 1308 B.S. (April 1901), the marriage of Aurobindo and Mrinalini was held at then Calcutta, according to religious and social codes of Hinduism- in the presence of distinguished persons like Lord Satyendra Prasad Sinha, Barrister Bomkesh Chakraborty, and Sri Jagadish Chandra Bose.[11] At this occasion, Smt. Nirod Mohini Devi, the wife of Girish Chandra and a poet of that period, wrote a poem 'Mrinale- Aurobindo' that expressed significance of this marriage as the manifestation of the eternal relation of divinity. She evaluated this divine relation between Mrinalini and Aurobindo thus:

> "...making them as One Life,
> In the Oneness of eternal Unity."[12]

The idea of the divine or eternal unity, expressed through the married life of Aurobindo, explains the proper meaning and Indian view of marriage which is not for mere material and biological satisfactions but for the service of others, expressing an intimate relation of unity with all. This wider and social outlook helps the couple to enter into their family life which makes them conscious about their social interests, over and above their individual demands. This represents the social significance of family life where men are conscious of social responsibilities and are also trained for social service. In this context, we may refer to the opinion of sociologists like Gillin and Blackmar who observe in family-the fundamentals of social life, where '...people are trained for larger social life'.[13]

This wider view, transcending family life, established through marriage as divine or human relation, can be expressed through its social approach to life by gradually detaching oneself–from the narrow and individual interests. This social or humanitarian view thus gradually inspire Aurobindo to assert his existence in the larger social life that finally urges him to search for the highest being of man in this world. In the background of this analysis of Aurobindo's life and outlook, it is found that the human relation of love finally appears as divine relation of unity, which, according to Aurobindo, appears as *Bhavani* or Mother, that is, an invocation for an Infinite Energy or *Shakti*. This Energy in man inspires him to transcend his limitation or finiteness in life for the development of Infiniteness in him that finally leads him to search for a Universal Unity with all. It may be noted in this connection that this power or *Shakti* as Universal Unity, as Aurobindo observes, is the fundamental basis of life that unites all the ways and methods of life like knowledge, love, and action and makes life creative through the introduction of harmony in the evolutionary progress of the individual and the social existences of man. This realisation of *Shakti* thus urged Aurobindo to transcend his narrow attachment or desire and inspire him to sacrifice his poor interest for others. This feeling of Aurobindo gave rise to a feeling of detachment from his family life. His objective became to realise a life for and with others, that is, to work for the freedom of Mankind in general, and this way, he began to feel that his existence in family and society was due to the welfare of the country and the countrymen initially, because these, according to him, were the expressions of a transcendent divine energy pervasively present in humanity as a whole. Aurobindo expressed this feeling before his wife and wrote; - "...I have three madness. Firstly, it is my firm faith, that whatever virtue, talent, higher education and knowledge and wealth which God has given me, belongs to Him....

The second folly has recently taken hold of me; it is this: by whatever means I must get the direct realisation of the Lord....

The third folly is this: Whereas others regard the country as an inert object, and know it as the plains, the fields, the forests, the mountains and rivers, I look upon my country as the mother, I worship her and adore her as the mother...."[14]

An intense feeling for this transcendent universal outlook and selflessness for humanity and for country and countrymen urged Aurobindo to engage himself directly for the socio-political freedom of motherland, which, according to him, was the direct expression of *Shakti* as Mother in and through him.

References

1. P. Nagaraja Rao, Contemporary Indian Philosophy, p. 93.
2. Sri Aurobindo, Collected Poems and Plays, I, p. 34.
3. Sri Aurobindo, Karmayogin, number VII.
4. Santi Nath Chattopadhyay, Art. 'Sri Aurobinder Darshane Manush O Somaj', Betar Jagat, AIR, Calcutta, p. 591.
5. K.R. Srinivasa Iyengar, Sri Aurobindo, p. 24.
6. A.B. Purani, The Life of Sri Aurobindo (1872-1926), p. 7.
7. *Ibid*, p. 28.
8. Sri Aurobindo, On Himself, p.13.
9. Sri Aurobindo, Collected Poems and Plays. Vol. I, p.18.
10. Sri Aurobindo, On *Yoga*, II, Tome I, p.129.
11. Santi Nath Chattopadhyay, Art., 'Mrinale-Aurobindo', the Souvenir of Vidyutchakra Sadharan Pathagar, Dumdum, Kolkata.
12. *Ibid*, p. 7.
13. Gillin and Blackmar, Outline of Sociology, pp. 186-188.
14. Letter to Mrinalini, 30th August, 1905.

    *This translated letter to Mrinalini, and other letters were taken away by police at the time of searching the Gray Street house in relation to the Alipore trial.

Part - II

Importance of the Integral Idea of Revolutionary Nationalism in the Freedom of Man and Motherland

Man is born in a society and this free existence may be called as his socio-political freedom. But his bondage in the society is due to different types of exploitations which are responsible for this suppression of his universal nature. The expression of this nature in man, is found very much normal and natural, that, according to Aurobindo, is the opening of the Universal Energy or *Shakti* in the individual and social life as the expression of the religion of Man in society. *Shakti* in the individual existence, expresses his infiniteness, and *Shakti* in the social existence as a nation is the infinite power of the millions of people.

In the background of this analysis, Aurobindo took his motherland as *Bhavani Bharati* or *Shakti* of the millions of people. But she was weak, inactive and was also under bondage due to the weakness and ignorance of her people. So for the freedom of India, Aurobindo observes, the awakening of the power or *Shakti* is very much necessary, which, according to him, is religious awakening of people as the expression of the proper nature or religion of men and nation, developing unity and universality.

Thus, it may be noted here that for the social freedom of India, Aurobindo wanted the religious awakening and Spiritual Regeneration of India for the awakening of the Universal Spirit or Infinite Energy in the heart of Indians. In this process, India was not taken as a land or country but was taken as mother or *Shakti*; and for the re-establishment of the traditional way of life as the expression of India's religious or spiritual outlook, the development of self-respect and respect for our own country and countrymen also were necessary. These were the fundamental factors of the religion of nation as the basis of the philosophical outlook of *Indian Nationalism*.

For the introduction of this national outlook in the heart of the countrymen, Aurobindo Ghosh took an active part in the national movement of India. In 1904, he was present at the Congress and in 1906, he took a significant role in the counsels of the Extremist party and then after his arrival at Calcutta he joined as the Principal of National College at Calcutta, founded in August, 1906. Being a nationalist he took an important part in Nationalist party and became the editor of national paper, *Bandemataram*, started by Bepin Chandra Pal. Through this daily paper, Aurobindo Ghosh circulated the objects, nature, ways, social significance, religious or philosophical basis of *Nationalism*. In order to understand the contributions of Aurobindo on the development of this idea, its nature and characters are to be evaluated briefly, developed under the guidance of different leaders and social reformers.

In the development of the ideal of *Nationalism* in Bengal the important and valuable contributions of Raja Ram Mohan Roy and Vidyasagar may be referred to. They thought about the reformation of society through the influence of Western education and culture. In this connection it may be said that the *'Young Bengal'* of Ramagopal Ghosh and *'Brahmo Samaj'* founded by Ram Mohan Roy, created influence on the growth of the national spirit in Bengal. For the inauguration of national outlook in society, Jyotirindranath Tagore established *'Sanjivani Sabha'* and Acharya Rajnarayan Basu was its President and Rabindranath Tagore was one of its important members. For the fulfillment of this purpose, Nabagopal Mitra, Dijendranath Tagore and others started *'Hindu Mela'* or *'Chaitra Mela'* about which Gaganendranath Tagore remarked, 'our union is not for ordinary religion and work....It is for our own country, for India'. For the expression of the same idea through the circulation of the national ideals and characters of national hero like Shivaji, the great Maharastrian writer and reformer Sakharam Ganesh Deuskar started '*Shivaji Mahotsav*', and with this '*Shivajir Mahattva*' in 1903, '*Shivaji*' with '*Shivajir Diksha*' of Rabindranath in 1906 and '*Shivaji*' were published for the inauguration of national spirit in young mind. In 1871, B.S. Shibnath Shastri with Dwarakanath Chattopadhyay, Durgamohan Das, and others formed a secret society, the object of which was 'The establishment of a great Republic in the world, through the foundation of Justice over injustice, equality over inequality, the power of the people over the power of the king.'

This process of growing the national spirit took a shape of *Nationalism* through the writings and thoughts on '*Anandamath*', '*Devi Chowdhurani*' of Bankim Chandra, '*Bharat Sangit*' of Hemchandra, '*Svapnalabdha-Bharatvarser Itihas*' of Bhudeb Mukhopadhyay, '*Deser Katha*' of Sakharam Ganesh Deuskar, etc.

The fundamental object of this outlook of *Nationalism* was to found this ideal on religion where Swami Vivekananda introduced a revolutionary ideal and expressed his desire before Sakharam that he wanted to observe revolution in India in his life time.[1] The revolutionary outlook of *Religious Nationalism* introduced by Swamiji, was accepted by Indian Nationalists, Extremists, Terrorists, and also respected him as '*National hero*'.

This revolutionary outlook of *Nationalism* was going to be gradually applied in practical work and for this purpose and for conducting the revolutionary work, Nivedita, a direct disciple of Vivekananda, formed a '*National Council*'. This process was developed perfectly through the introduction of *Revolutionary Nationalism* by Aurobindo Ghosh, which was to unite the idea of *Nationalism* as theory with the revolutionary work in practice.

If the nature of the *Revolutionary Nationalism* is properly examined, it is found that it grows from the heart of the country in relation with the tradition, culture and Indian way of life and is developed in a systematic manner through the contributions of different national leaders. To explain its harmonious nature and evolutionary progress, Aurobindo evaluates its significance in its relation with the nature and development of man for his freedom.

In the analysis of the *Revolutionary Nationalism*, it is found that it stands on the development of excellence or glory of our own country, which, according to Aurobindo, is to respect our country as mother or *Shakti*. It, as he observes, requires the revival of *Hinduism* or *Sanatana Dharma* for the establishment of the relation of unity of *Nationalism* with the Indian tradition, culture and way of life which finally leads to Spiritual Regeneration of India. The fundamental object of this process is to explain *Nationalism* as religion of people or nation, because the religion of Man is the expression of the infinite power, and religion of nation is the expression of the power of the millions of people; and *Nationalism,* in this sense, is the inauguration of power or *Shakti* in the heart of Indians for their socio-political freedom. In the light of this evaluation, Aurobindo finally explained the nature and character of *Nationalism* as religion or *dharma.*

Nationalism as religion or *dharma*, is finally expressed as *Revolutionary Nationalism*, which develops respect in man as the realisation of power and also increases respect for the country as the mother or *Shakti*. In 1905, Aurobindo Ghosh wrote a book on '*Bhavani Mandir*' where he expressed that for the freedom of motherland, India would be worshipped as *Bhavani* or *Shakti* that required the sacrifice of a group of workers who had a similarity with the ideals and disinterested service of the organised political monks of '*Anandamath*' of Bankimchandra. This idea created a tremendous influence on the minds of the educated young people of Bengal, who became gradually interested in India and about her tradition, culture, religion and philosophy. To create this respect about the tradition as the Indian way of life, Aurobindo Ghosh and Bipinchandra Paul formed '*Arya Samaj*' and its fundamental objects were the reformations of *Hinduism* and Hindu Society and to organise movements for the freedom of Hindustan.

So in this way the ideal of *Revolutionary Nationalism* stood on the revival of *Hinduism* or *Sanatana Dharma* for the establishment of the relation of unity of *Nationalism* with the Indian tradition and Indian way of life. The significance of this unity lies in the *Spiritual Regeneration* that is to explain the infinite power of man as divine and free. In order to explain this nature of man and his freedom,

Aurobindo Ghosh evaluated the ideas of *Vedas, Upanishads, Geeta* and other traditional Indian thoughts that represented the idea of Man as Universal. Following this clue, Aurobindo Ghosh interpreted the gods and goddesses of *Veda* as the expressions of multiple powers of the one Divine, who is realised by different men in different forms. This, according to Aurobindo, is a kind of monotheism within which the monistic, pantheistic and polytheistic vision of the cosmic reality is included. Aurobindo explains it as "...a system of parallelism by which the same deities were at once internal and external powers of Universal Nature, and they managed its expression through a system of double values by which the same language served for their worship in both aspects"[2] In this explanation, it is observed that Vedic idea of God as the Divine Being is expressed through different forms of infinite power that refers to the divinity or infiniteness of man in this world. Aurobindo observes this integral vision of man and God in *Upanishads*, where he finds the expression of *integral monism* instead of *monism* or *theism.* In this *integral monism* of *Upanishads,* it is found that the man, being a part of the divine manifestation in the world and his inner self is united with the *Supreme Self* or *Brahman.*[3] Thus, in the light of Upanishads, Aurobindo observes that man in this world, is in individualised being who is potentially *Divine* or *Universal* and can express his Divine power in the evolution of his worldly existence in freedom.

This idea of the evolution of divine or infinite existence of man is evaluated by Aurobindo, in the context of the *Geeta,* that, according to him is a pragmatic synthesis of the ideas of *Sankhya* and *Yoga* under *Vedantic* structure. Man, in this sense, is an individual divine who evolves in this world of nature for the expression of divinity in his fighting for freedom for unity in existence.[4]

Evaluating the free and infinite power of man in the light of traditional thought and religion of India, Aurobindo explains the essential nature of man as the expression of this power in his freedom which is his fundamental religion of life and thus in the light of this evaluation of human life, he also explains the eternal spirit of the collective life of man as the '*soul of the nation*' which expresses the infinite power of the millions of people in society as the religion of nation or *Nationalism*. So, *Nationalism,* being the '*larger national self*', Aurobindo explains it as religion or *Dharma* that expresses the divinity in social life. He observes, "...nationalism is a religion that has come from God."[5]

As *Nationalism* expresses the divine power of people in society, it is immortal and eternal and spontaneously works in human nature for his freedom in society. Aurobindo writes, "Nationalism is immortal, nationalism cannot die because it is no human thing, it is God who is working in Bengal. God cannot be killed, God cannot be sent to jail."[6]

Thus, *Nationalism*, being an eternal national self, the realisation of '*the Soul of Society*'[7] in the social freedom of man is fundamentally required through the socio-moral methods or techniques. For this purpose, Aurobindo emphasized the importance and necessity of *Sadhana* as the method of spiritual identification with the spiritual energy or *Shakti*, and *jnana* as the realisation of spiritual vision of unity through the transcendence of ego or poor self-interest. The introduction of these traditional and spiritual methods through *Yoga of Jnana*, *Bhakti* and *Karma* were to make the brain and character of the nation to be spiritually revolutionised.[8] Thus, in this process, it was found that the ideal of *Nationalism* as theory was introduced in practice through different revolutionary activities that established *Nationalism* as the *Revolutionary Nationalism* which is the synthesis of the eternal spirit of renunciation in the idea of revolution with the application of this universal spirit in practice. Zacharias rightly observes, "Nationalism in India today is the sweet harmony between the new ideal of Mazzini and the old ideal of Sannyasa"[9], which requires "the real self-sacrifice in the cause of the Motherland." In this context of the evaluation, we find the similarity of the national and revolutionary ideas of Mazzini and Aurobindo. But it should be noted in this connection that Aurobindo's idea of *Revolutionary Nationalism* as the religion of nation comes from the evolutionary progress of the Indian tradition or Indian outlook of *Dharma* that includes socio-political, moral, intellectual, and spiritual works of men.

Thus, evaluating the idea of *Nationalism* as religion Aurobindo explained it as *Revolutionary Nationalism* which was introduced in the practical life in Society through the different revolutionary activities. In 1901-02, P. Mitra with others established a permanent and a secret committee *'Anusheelan Samiti'* for revolutionary works in Bengal and Aurobindo Ghosh became its Acharya and his brother Barindra Kumar became its chief organiser. Regarding the importance and necessity of revolutionary activities, Aurobindo wrote, "It was P. Mitra and Miss Ghosal who started it at the inspiration of Baron Okakura. They had already started and when I visited Bengal I came to know about it. I simply kept myself informed of their work. My idea was an armed revolution in the whole of India."[10] This revolutionary outlook of Aurobindo was gradually circulated in the country through the national papers '*Bandemataram*', '*Karmayogin*' and '*Dharma*', edited by him and was expressed in Bengal in an extreme stage when on the 3rd December of 1903, Lord Carzon declared the partition of Bengal. For a strong protest against this declaration, '*Banga Bhanga*' movement as a direct challenge to the authoritarianism of the alien government, was started in Bengal, under the leadership of the revolutionary nationalists Aurobindo Ghosh and Bipin Chandra Pal. Kingsford, the Presidency Magistrate of Calcutta, came forward to suppress this movement and two youngmen Khudiram Basu and Prafulla Chaki of Revolutionary group went after Kingsford and on 30th April, 1908, Khudiram threw a bomb for murdering him and was failure. On 11th August, Khudiram was hanged and on 1st May of 1908, Prafulla Chaki committed suicide. In connection with this happening as the Muzaffarpur murder, Aurobindo Ghosh was arrested on 3rd May, 1908, and Barindra Kumar and other revolutionary nationalists also were arrested in different places and with reference to this arrest the famous *Alipore Bomb Trial* was started.

In the analysis of the evolutionary progress of the idea of *Nationalism* towards the establishment of the *Revolutionary Nationalism* as the religion of nation, the Alipore Bomb case was very much important and significant; because through this Bomb case, India acquired two other great revolutionary nationalists, Deshbandhu Chittaranjan Das and Netaji Subhas Chandra Bose, who were the real successors of the revolutionary outlook of Swami Vivekananda and Sri Aurobindo.

It is observed that through the contributions and activities of these leaders and reformers, Aurobindo's idea of *Nationalism* as the religion of nation and its method of application of revolutionary spirit as *Revolutionary Nationalism*, evaluated significantly the chief principles and fundamental objects of this national outlook for the acquirement of political freedom through the expulsion of foreign rule for the political independence of the countrymen in his own country and then it is also for the social freedom for equality and social justice for the development of free and internal relationship among them in his own motherland.

In this context it may also be noted here that in the history of Indian Independence, the *Alipore Bomb case* is also very much significant in another sense. Through this Bomb trial, India also discovered another Aurobindo, who, in the process of synthesis of India's national or spiritual outlook with the revolutionary method of *Yoga* or meditation, realised the universal unity within him, through this realisation Aurobindo Ghosh, a man, the individual gradually became Sri Aurobindo, The Man, The Universal. On the 6th May of 1909, according to the delivery of judgement by Mr Beachroft, Aurobindo Ghosh was acquitted but Sri Aurobindo in him at that time, tried the searching for the real significance of the *Revolutionary Nationalism* towards the establishment of the spiritual or internal freedom through an integral or integral process of *Yoga* for the development of perfect unity in human life and a complete harmony in human society as the expression of divine life in man and society.

In and through the continuous progress of the revolutionary spirit of Universality in the evolutionary progress of his existence as the religion or expression of the universal nature of life, Sri Aurobindo arrived at Pondicherry on the 4th April of 1910 and gradually started another revolutionary process of meditation or *Yoga* for the establishment of the inner or spiritual freedom in unity as the expression of the divinity in man through a synthesis of his material, social and spiritual states of existence as the state of integrality.

References

1. Dr Bhupendranath Dutta, Bharater Dvitiya Svadhinata Samgram.
2. Sri Aurobindo, The Secret of the Veda, 1971, p. 30.
3. Sri Aurobindo, Isha Upanishads, 1973.
4. Sri Aurobindo, Life Divine, I.
5. Sri Aurobindo, Speeches, pp.7-8.
6. *Ibid*, pp. 8-9.
7. Sri Aurobindo, The Ideal of Human Unity, p. 224.
8. Sri Aurobindo, The Brain of India, p. 8.
9. Zacharias, Renascent India, p. 149.
10. Letter, December 18, 1938.

Part - III

The Significance of Integral View in Developing Unity in Man and Society

A careful examination of the life history of Sri Aurobindo through different periods of student life, married life, political life and spiritual life, proves that the progress of his life is continuous, as one stage of life is intimately related with the other stage and also is integral as it synthesises the fundamental ideals of Indian tradition and culture, in the background of the scientific outlook of Western civilisation. It cultivates a proper revolutionary spirit with the revolutionary method of application of this idea in life and society. This integral development of his life leads to the inauguration of an integral outlook for the explanation of the universal existence of man as his essential religion of life in society. This may be evaluated as the expression of the nature of individual's life and his collective life as the religion of nation that finally leads to the development of unity or harmony in human life and society.

In this analysis of the integral outlook of Sri Aurobindo, it is observed that it explains the material, social and spiritual existences of man integrally that evaluates the political, social and spiritual freedom of men in a integral manner.

As man exists in this material world, so his material existence is free and independent of any conditions, imposed by others upon the essential or natural progress of his life. These external impositions on human life break the continuity in the progress of life and also may create limitations and contradictions in society.

These limitations or contradictions may be due to exploitations by others which may be recognised as the political exploitations and these are also due to social inequalities, injustice, etc. The elimination of these socio-political hindrances on the natural development of life, leads to the social and political freedom of man in society that is interpreted by Sri Aurobindo as the expression of religion and *Dharma* and for which he introduces the *Revolutionary Nationalism* as the synthesis of the national ideal and revolutionary method.

But the fundamental object of this socio-political freedom of men, in the observation of Sri Aurobindo, is the introduction of the spiritual or internal freedom for the development of Universality, in and through the development of intimate and essential relation of unity in all and also is for the freedom from all types of alienations and exploitations.

Sri Aurobindo evaluates his idea of freedom as the synthesis of the Eastern and Western Culture. He points out that socio-political freedom of man is the result of the progress of the Western civilisation and the idea of internal or spiritual freedom is evolved from the progress of Eastern Culture.

In the evaluation of the socio-political freedom in the light of Western civilisation, it may be noted that this idea of freedom, according to Dr Varma, was grown and developed under the guidance and valuable contributions of different thinkers in different periods like the socio-moral concept of freedom or idea of Eleutheria developed by Plato, Aristotle and other Greek thinkers, the ideas of equality and fellow relationship of Stoics, reformative view of Christian thinkers, social equality of Karl Marx, coming out of capitalistic form of Economy, ideas of natural rights in the Seventeenth century gradually gave birth to the consciousness of democratic rights and liberty. Regarding the importance of these contributions in the development of the western outlook of socio-political freedom, Dr Varma rightly observes, "Thus we can distinguish these five broad currents and philosophic movements in the evolution of the European concept of the political and social liberty of man–the Hellenic concept of Eleutheria, Stoicism, Christianity and Reformation, the capitalistic system of economy, and the theory of natural rights and social contract."[1]

However, the fundamental object of the socio-political freedom of man, as developed in the thoughts of the West, is to assert the material existence of man in socio-economic and socio-political form of liberty.

Sri Aurobindo also is conscious of the socio-political freedom of man but the significance of his outlook of freedom lies in the development of his integral outlook of internal or spiritual freedom as the reconciliation of western approach to the external freedom and the Indian approach to the inner freedom of man. He writes, "They (the Europeans) have found out the way to the external freedom. We have found out the way to internal freedom. We meet and give to each other what we have gained. We have learned from them to aspire after external as they will learn from us to aspire after internal freedom."[2] The significance of this programme lies in the real development of equality in man and society. In this connection, Sri Aurobindo points out, "...we learned from them (the Europeans) to strive after political equality and in return for what they have given us we shall lead them to the secret of the equality within."[3]

The social and spiritual significance of this idea of equality lies in its synthesis of the external and the internal freedom that is finally evaluated in Sri Aurobindo's idea of spiritual freedom as the freedom in unity.

In the application of this idea in the socio-political life of man and nation, Sri Aurobindo emphasised the Indian traditional idea of *Swaraj* as the growth of the nation from within for freedom in unity within and without as national self-dependence or self-help which is different from *Swadhinata* as mere political independence. In the light of this observation, Gandhiji also points out that, "The word *Swaraj* is a sacred word, a Vedic word, meaning self-rule and self-restraint, and not freedom from all restraint which independence often means."[4]

Thus, the analysis of the freedom in the background of the Indian thought, explains integrally the true significance of human freedom in life and society, that, in the observation of Sri Aurobindo, is a synthesis of both outer and inner freedom of man for the freedom in unity of material, social and spiritual existence of human beings.

It may be noted in this context that the integral development of Sri Aurobindo's idea of freedom as the freedom in unity, finally explains the real significance of the human existence, free from within and without for the introduction of equality and unity which is to be developed through the human realisation. Sri Aurobindo writes, "The union of liberty and equality can only be achieved by the power of human brotherhood and it cannot be founded on anything else...."[5]

Thus, it is observed that the proper importance of freedom for equality finally lies in the development of human relation. Rabindranath, another contemporary Indian thinker, also emphasises the importance of the growth and the development of humanity or human relation for the explanation of the history of human freedom. In *'The Religion of Man'*, Tagore observes thus, 'The history of the growth of freedom is the history of the perfection of human relationship.' So the significance of this outlook lies in the inauguration of humanity and development of human relation in the world. In the evaluation of this ideal, Sri Aurobindo points out that this ideal of humanity cannot be properly explained in the context of mere material existence of man, but on the other hand it is spiritual as it synthesises the material and universal existence of man through the inauguration of divinity in him. It makes the material existence of man significant, through a reconciliation of all material contradictions like socio-political, socio-moral, socio-cultural contradictions into unity, and establishes the real freedom in unity, in individual, social or national and even in international life in this world.

In the light of this idea, Sri Aurobindo explained his desires, evaluating the significance of unity of the Independence Day of India on his seventy-seventh birthday, when he expressed that he had three dreams, -one was to create such revolution through which India would be united and become free, the second was of the re-awakening and freedom of Asia and the third was of world unity.

For the introduction of the idea of social unity in his concept of socio-political freedom of Mother India, Sri Aurobindo thought of the introduction of the *Revolutionary Nationalism* in India. Similarly for the world unity, he emphasised the importance of spiritual freedom as the unity of external and internal freedom of man for the divine life on earth through the inauguration of humanity, in and through another revolutionary process of *Integral Yoga* as a new integral discipline for growing from within.

Thus, in the context of the analysis of the continuous progress of Sri Aurobindo's life and insightful-integral development of his thought, it is observed that its fundamental object is to explain the true significance of man in the unity of his material and spiritual existence which is eternal and universal. The expression of this universality in man is his proper religion of Man which is not to ignore his material existence but to make his material existence more significant and organised through the reconciliation of material contradictions for the real freedom in unity in and through the development of the human relationship as the *religion of humanity*. In the evaluation of this integral idea and its integral development, Sri Aurobindo writes, "A *religion of humanity* means the growing realisation that there is a secret Spirit, a divine Reality, in which we are all one, the humanity is its highest present vehicle on earth, that the human race and the human being are the means by which it will progressively reveal itself here."[6]

Thus, the introduction of this outlook of the *religion of humanity* as the expression of the divinity, is to manifest the divine life on earth for human unity which is to attain peace and perfection, potential in human life as truth. He writes, "...the higher hope of humanity lies in the growing number of men who will realise this truth and seek to develop it in themselves, so that when the mind of man is ready to escape from its mechanical-bent, -perhaps when it finds that its mechanical solutions are all temporary and disappointing, -the truth of the Spirit may step in and lead humanity to the path of its highest possible happiness and perfection."[7]

In the light of this idea of the 'truth of The Spirit' as the integral development of divinity and humanity as 'perfection' in man, Sri Aurobindo evaluates the eternal nature and universal existence of man as the religion of Man, The Universal, over and above the limitations and contradictions in life and world.

References

1. Dr V P Varma, The Political Philosophy of Sri Aurobindo, p. 356.
2. Sri Aurobindo, Speeches, p. 115.
3. *Ibid*, p. 117.
4. M. Desai, With Gandhiji in Ceylon, p. 93.
5. Sri Aurobindo, The Ideal of Human Unity, pp. 268-9.
6. Sri Aurobindo and The Mother on Human Unity, p. 25.
7. *Ibid*, p. 27.

Chapter - 2

The Meaning and Nature of the Philosophy of Religion: An Integral Development of Divinity in Man and World

Part - I

The Religion and Religionism

The growth and the development of the integral and humanitarian view of Sri Aurobindo, through a continuous and evolutionary progress of his life and thought, finally evaluate the socio-political, socio-cultural and spiritual significance of the human existence in an integral manner, that explains the universal nature and existence of man as the proper religion of his life, where he finds the existence of man in religion and religion in Man.

In the context of this integral outlook of Sri Aurobindo, the meaning and nature of the idea of the religion is to be evaluated in order to explain the significance and character of his idea of religion as the religion in Man.

The proper evaluation of the meaning and the nature of the term religion and the proper examination of the nature and existence of man prove that there is a close and intimate relation of man with religion. Man exists in the limitations of the material world and society and his fundamental object in his social life is to become free from limitations or contradictions in society, not by ignoring these contradictions but through their reconciliation in unity. In the context of this analysis it may be said that the religion is intimate with the human life as the expression of human nature. The term 'religion' is derived from the Latin word 'religare' as a 'bond' which is to be interpreted by different thinkers as natural, social or spiritual union in life in contradictions. The Sanskrit meaning of the term 'religion' as '*dharma*' is also derived from the unity of '*Dhridhatu*' with '*Man pratyaya*', the internal meaning of which is the introduction of the greater unity in social life of man through the harmonisation of his external and internal nature.

Thus, the meaning of religion as the principle of unification, may be evaluated that socially as the development of the relation of man with others in society through the establishment of the social coherency. For the proper evaluation of this social meaning of religion as social relation of unity, it is finally explained by Sri Aurobindo in a deeper or spiritual sense as the divine relation and the development of this relation in society is to develop the divinity in man as the unity of the idea of God and man in the individual and the social existence of human beings for the introduction of divine life on earth.

But this sense of religion as the religion of divinity is negated by different thinkers and for the predominance of divine spirit in the inner essence of religion, its existence or importance is also ignored by them. All these thinkers emphasise the importance and the reality of matter in this world and so human life is purely material and thus social relation, according to them, is nothing but the material or mechanical relation. The development of this thought in nineteenth century, gives rise to the theories of (a) *Dogmatic Naturalism or Materialism*, (b) *Agnostic Naturalism,*[1] (c) *Psychological Naturalism*, and all these theories are treated as *Naturalism* because all these theories explain the human life as natural or material which is opposed to the supernatural or spiritual outlook.

In modern times, *Positivism* and *Marxism* also hold the same opinion and emphasise the material existence of man which is to be explained socially from the socio-economic, socio-political and socio-cultural sense. Religion, is taken by these thinkers as the imposition of something on the material or the natural existence of man, and thus it is used for the exploitation of the people. For this, Marx[2] explains it as 'the opium of the people' and Comte[3], the founder of *Positivism*, denounces this type of religion as something non-human or super-human and thus he puts a supreme importance on the existence of man and so introduces the *religion of humanity*.

After a careful observation of the Indian outlook of religion as the expression of human nature and existence, it is observed that it is to be evaluated by Sri Aurobindo and other contemporary Indian thinkers as the essential process of religion of Man in development. In this sense, it is found that mere explanation of human nature as material and mechanical something, makes man limited and more finite, which is responsible for creating contradictions in life and society. These thinkers, on the other hand, put an importance on the infinite or divine nature of man that makes his existence in this material world more significant. But it should be noted in this connection that Indian *spiritualism*, as examined by Sri Aurobindo and others, is not statically supernatural and so does not ignore the confronted material existence of man which has to be construed as a process-but the spiritual view of Sri Aurobindo entertains the confronted material order and transcendent divine or spiritual order as insightful experiential process that makes him more creative in society, fostering a ground for a novel, intimate or human relationship among men, for the final accomplishment in unity.

This idea of the religion in the making as the religion of Man, projects the experience of religion to a perspective order with man as the transforming agent of natural or material orders to reach the insightful requirements of divine orders of existence for unifying the process between God and man. Sri Aurobindo explains the significance of this realistic divinity in life as very vital one which is the Reality or Truth of human life that is to be realisable divinity in life as very vital one which is the Reality or Truth of human life that is to be realised in life for the transcendence of imperfections. He writes, "In order to exceed our nature and become divine, we must first get God; for we are the lower imperfect term of our being, He, its higher perfect term. The finite, to become infinite, must know, love and touch infinity; the symbol being in order to become its own reality, must know, love and perceive that Reality."[4] Hence, Sri Aurobindo's was an insightful transforming process.

A careful analysis of the existence of man, in the context of this dynamic notion of Reality, it is to be observed that the significance of the human life lies in the realisation of this Reality that leads to a gradual manifestation of divinity in the evolution of different stages of human existence towards the completeness as the focal unity in confronting the apparent contradictions in life and society.

This progressive insightfully transforming notion of Reality or Truth, as manifested in the different stages of life as the expression of religious or spiritual experience, is explained and experimented by the different human approaches to Reality, like Science, Philosophy and Religion, etc. All these branches of human knowledge in process-can reveal the particular aspect of Truth or Reality focused in a particular point of view. Thus, it is observed that philosophy is a critical evaluation of Reality in process and so it satisfies human reason in its adventure-postulating a divine union, and this satisfies at once our emotional and rational demands as of a science demanding observation and the experiments, to determine the strength of Truth as expressed in life and society in a practical form.

But in the analysis of the proper nature of man and the significance of his existence in society, the observations of all the branches of human knowledge are to be evaluated integrally with progressive insights for a systematic and harmonious explanation of human life towards a progressive completeness. In the light of this observation, Sri Aurobindo evaluates the contributions of these branches of thought prospectively for the explanation of the totality of being as the expression of divinity as an integral process. He writes, "To get at this as a spiritual presence is the aim of religion, to grow into harmony with its nature of light, love, strength and purity is the aim of ethics, to enjoy and would ourselves into the harmony of its eternal beauty and delight is the aim and consummation of our aesthetic need and nature, to know and to be according to its eternal principles of truth is the end of Science and Philosophy and of all our insistent drive towards knowledge."[5] Thus, in the opinion of Sri Aurobindo, this prospectively oriented explanation of different branches of knowledge in the context of the divine integrality can be significantly expressed as the potential unity in man through the expression of his potential nature in the unity of his reason, emotion and action in life. The realisation and the manifestation of this integral psychic process in transformation at developments–constitutes–the divine unity in life and action, according to Sri Aurobindo, is the 'highest secret' of man to realise-which is to be explained by the different adventures of his thought in a prospectively oriental sphere. Sri Aurobindo writes, "Science takes possession of the measures and utilities of force, rational philosophy pursues reason to its last subtleties, but inspired philosophy and religion can seize hold of the highest secret, *uttamam rahasyam*."[6] Thus, in the light of this analysis it may be said that the discovery of this 'highest secret' in man is the fundamental objective of all branches of human knowledge, like Science, Philosophy and Religion- in their prospective pursuits.

In this observation of Sri Aurobindo, it is found that the knowledge and the realisation of this 'highest secret' in life and existence, is a dynamic possibility for human as piration, which is "....his seeking for perfection, his longing for freedom and mastery, his search after pure truth and unmixed delight–is in flagrant contradiction with his present existence and normal experience."[7]

In the analysis of the human nature, Sri Aurobindo observes that there is a conflict or contradiction as the essential part of human life which is coming out of its dependence on his material existence. As man exists in this material world, his mere desire for the satisfaction of mere material needs or individual interests subjects one to a self-created limitation or finiteness in terms of one's '*ego*' which clashes with the social interest. But the significance of the human life, lies, not with this contradiction, but with resolving of it through one's realisation of harmony; where man, in the opinion of N. Bohr, exists as 'both spectator and actor'. L. Barnet evaluates this view thus: "For man by the very condition of his being, is his finiteness and involvement in nature. The further he extends his horizons, the more vividly he recognises the fact that, as the physicist Niels Bohr puts it, 'we are both spectators and actors in the great drama of existence'. Man is thus his own greatest mystery."[8] This is explained as a belonging to a dual order-of Seer-Seen process.

This 'greatest mystery' is the 'highest secret' of man, according to Sri Aurobindo. He expresses it through his notion of evolution of human existence in this world, where man evolves by an inner transformation, realising harmony and peace.

The harmony to Sri Aurobindo is not an accidental factor, but on the other hand, it is an essential part of the evolution of human life, that presents the co-existence of man's–material and social existence. Man, in a higher centre of his life, transforms his natures to his material, social and spiritual nature, where there is an enjoyment of a unity of material, social and spiritual processes of life which elevate man to a transcendent order.

In the evolutionary progress of unity or harmony in life and society, -Sri Aurobindo evaluates its significance of the progressively emergent orders of life from matter, and mind from life, and both these evolved orders, are later elevated to a transcendent divine or spiritual order of nature as the manifestation of a potential power of consciousness that reveals the highest aspiration of man for the spiritual freedom in the insightful unity of basic orders of universe as a whole.

Thus, in the observation of Sri Aurobindo, it is found that man's transcendent consciousness- is the highest state of evolution and the significance of this superb state- lie in the evolution of super consciousness in him that works for the development of divinity in life as unifying the transcendent possibilities beyond the basic-material, social and spiritual states of life. So, the significance of human existence in the final state of evolution lies in the manifestation of the supra consciousness as the realisation or expression of potential perfection or divinity in Man. In the light of this analysis it may be said that the evolution of human life is not complete through the mere material and biological progress in their line or orders of aspects, but in their emergent in mental and supramental order's to an Integral Consciousness. Huxley evaluates this transcendent supra-mental process thus: "Man's evolution is not biological but psychosocial; it operates by the mechanism of cultural tradition, which involves the cumulative self-reproduction and self-variation of mental activities and their products. Accordingly, major steps in the human phase of evolution are achieved by breakthroughs to new dominant patterns of mental organisation of knowledge, ideas, and beliefs-ideological instead of physiological or biological organisation…."[9]

This post ideological development in human existence in this world, through the progress of his inner power of perfection, makes him more significant and creative. Rabindranath Tagore observes, "...man appeared and turned the course of this evolution from an indefinite march of physical aggrandizement to a freedom of a more subtle perfection. This has made possible his progress to become unlimited, and has enabled him to realise the boundless in his power."[10]

The realisation of this boundless power in man, in the opinion of Sri Aurobindo, is spiritual in the supramental aspect-as it helps him to overcome the limitations in the life and world through a transcendent pathway where the finiteness of each emergent order is superseded by an integral process, where all processes in their individuality has a satisfaction in the realisation of a common objective of each one is transcendence or excellence. Thus, the infiniteness or divinity in the finite existence of man in this world, is realised in all varieties of ways that brings out the universal nature of man as the evolution of the religious consciousness of Man. Sri Aurobindo explains thus: "... the aim of religion, -but not unhappily of the creeds and churches– is to further the great aim of Nature by pushing man towards his evolution"[11] So the proper end of religion, is to explain the natural development of human life towards a completeness that is to be expressed through the development of his total emergent transcendent possibilities.

In the background of this analysis, if we explain the different views of religion, given by different thinkers, we may find all these thinkers refer to a particular element of human nature and explain its predominance in human existence that expresses the fundamental character of religion as an experience in process and possibility.

Hegelians put an importance on the rational faculty of man and explain religion as the expression of reason or rational knowledge. This outlook of religion, though emphasises an important faculty of reason, still it ignores emotional and other faculties of human life. Similarly Ritschell, Schleiermacher and others emphasise the feeling element and explain religion as the expression of emotion. But they also avoid the rational and other faculties of man. In the same way Kant and other moralists refer to the importance of the moral will of man and emphasise the moral aspect of religion. But religion is something more than morality, which includes moral, social and spiritual duties of life. Bradley observes, "Morality in brief calls for an unattainable unity of its aspects, and, in its search for this, it naturally is led beyond itself into a higher form of goodness. It ends in what we may call religion."[12] Thus, religion finally is an emergent transcendent consciousness of solitude, to which tallies with William James' varieties of religious experiences- "as the feelings, acts and experiences of individual men in their solitude so far as they apprehend themselves to stand in relation to whatever they may consider the divine."[13] Though this definition emphasises the divine aspect of religion, still it ignores the objective approach to divinity through which a man acquires freedom through the transcendence of limitation or finiteness. For this Sri Aurobindo, in the modern period, emphasises the cosmic liberation, which is an establishment of an integral view of divine unity in all human beings.

The cognizance of this divine unity in human life and society is possible through the development of divine value in life. For this, Hoffding evaluates religion as '...the faith in the conservation of value'. But the nature of this value is not merely moral or social, but is broadly religious or spiritual value as the expression of the religion of divinity, which, in the observation of Alexander, "...is faith in Deity" that is to be evaluated by him as "...the sentiment that we are drawn towards Him and caught in the movement of the world to a higher level of experience."[14] This value of Alexander emphasises the value of divinity that refers to the faith in God which is not yet but the world as a whole is a Nisus towards it. But though all these observations refer to the faith in God as the conserver of value, still these explanations ignore the practical approach or the realisation of value in life. Alexander departs from the tradition already existing or realised God, his is a God in emergence, not yet, beyond all the emergent qualities, and beyond 'values' in human Mental and Social situation, if conceived in Alexander's way is a chase for a fresh emergent quality beyond all values, beyond all existing realised orders.

But religion, as the expression of the divine value, as Dr Maitra in this context, points out, religion refers to the "...faith in the realisation of value."[15] Thus, the fundamental object of religion is the realisation of value, which is divine as it combines the value with its existence in the idea of God, who as the highest value of life, is to be realised in the different stages of human life in different degrees towards unity or completeness. Thus, the idea of religion as the thought and the realisation of divine value, makes the human existence more significant that expresses the essential nature of man as the expression of divinity. Dr Radhakrishnan observes, "The need of religion, for a system of thought, for devotion to a cause which will give our fragile and fugitive existence significance and value does not require much elaborate argument. It is an intrinsic element of human nature."[16] In the light of this observation, it may be said that the religion is 'an intrinsic element of human nature', which finally leads to the development of the completeness as unity in life as the expression of goodness or the highest value of divinity. This is the final and fundamental end of religion which is to be evaluated by Sri Aurobindo, "the inmost essence of religion...is the search for God and finding God. Its aspiration is to discover the Infinite, the Absolute, the One, the Divine who is all these things and yet no abstraction but a Being. Its work is a sincere giving out of the true and ultimate relations between man and God, relations of unity, relations of differences, relations of an illuminated knowledge, an ecstatic love and delight, and absolute surrender and service, a casting of every part of our existence out of its normal status into an up rush of man toward the Divine and a descent of the Divine into man."[17]

In the context of this evaluation, Sri Aurobindo observes that the evolution of the history of man is the history of his religious consciousness- that is not confined to a single religion only that is the expression of a transcendent divine nature of man manifest in different experiential stages of life in a dual manner by a descent and ascent– descent is from a supramental order to the mental, vital and material- ascent is from the matter to mind and to the supramental order. In this way Sri Aurobindo finds the history of different religions as expression of the nature of the transcendent Divine Truth in different stages of human life from the lower to the higher and finally towards the highest stage of the development of truth as an integrally realisable possibility of each Man. He writes, "...this chequered history belongs to all human efforts and if it were to count against the truth and necessity of religion, would count also against the truth and necessity of every other line of human endeavour, against all man's action, his ideals, his thought, his art, his science."[18]

Limitation of Religion

The history of man, in the opinion of Sri Aurobindo, is the history of human efforts or all types of human actions that express the idea of prospective integral consciousness in ascent to descent. The religion, that contains the existence of man in different times, expressed through the different types of human actions, accept both unity and contradictions in life and society. But it should be noted in this connection that these complete activities of man that create mere conflicts and tensions, express the defective part of religion as restricted particular-or religion or its expression viz *Religionism* that does not explain the totality or completeness of man, but it only refers to a particular aspect of life as the expression of power of intellect or reason of a particular person, culture or country. Though reason is treated as the highest faculty of man as it helps him to guide himself and to guide nature, it also has a definite function that helps a man to enlighten his different experiences and also helps to develop faith and conviction for increasing consciousness, still its influence in life is 'partial and passionate' as it does not surrender to the pure truth but increases the contradictory or conflicting forces. In this way, Sri Aurobindo observes that restricted or abstract reason can never reach the supreme or final truth or reality which is infinite and complete in its expression from a transcendent centre in duality-descent and ascent in togetherness. A restricted reason only separates mere finites or facts.

Religion, which deals with the total prospective nature of man, where its fundamental object is to express the potential divinity through the development of an integral consciousness beyond all restricted processes from matter to mind-that can be explained by any restricted reason properly; as it deals with a focal point without a stretch of a before and after. It can never explain the nature of the transcendent divine possibility- the completeness of the nature and the existence of man in a superb transcendent religious process and possibility.

But Sri Aurobindo points out that the influence of this limited faculty of reason in man, compels him to observe the limitations or separations in life, responsible for producing evils or contradictions in society. Thus, this side of human life deals with the importance of artificialities, restrictions, impositions of dogmas, etc. on the natural and spontaneous development of human life and thus have created *Religionism* as contradictions, expressed in different types of religions, instead of developing the essential spirit of religion as the religion of Man or humanity.

Sri Aurobindo states that though religion acquired a central place in ancient time for its searching for truth, potent in the nature and existence of man, still the gradual influence of the partial faculty of reason in man, expressed through the *Religionism* or artificiality in religion, created orthodoxy, superstition, cruelty, etc. In this process, religion was guided for the fulfillment of individual interest or the particular interest of religious institutions or of different religions, instead of the integral cosmic-social interest for the development of human life and society. As a result of this process, a protest or reaction in the form of revolution was created in society and in every religious process- for the rejection of religion and thus different anti-religious theories and anti-God opinions were created or fostered in society.

According to Sri Aurobindo, the cause of this reaction against religion is for its intimacy with *Religionism*, that, in the one hand unites religion with the rigidities, dogmas and accidental rules and regulations; for Sri Aurobindo observes, "If religion has failed, it is because it has confused the essential with the adventitious. True religion is spiritual religion; it is a seeking after God, the opening of the deepest life of the soul to the indwelling Godhead, the eternal Omnipresence. Dogmas, cults, moral codes are aids and props; they may be offered to man but not imposed on him."[19] It, on the other hand, also takes religion as the renunciation and subjection of the passions and appetites by bodily severities which Sri Aurobindo points out, "Moreover, religion often considers spiritual as made up of renunciation and mortification. Religion thus becomes a force that discourages life and it cannot, therefore, be a true law and guide for life."[20]

Thus, Sri Aurobindo does not avoid or does not deny the defective part of religion which is very much harmful to mankind, but he does not accept this as the essential part of religion because, this, in the opinion of Sri Aurobindo, is to be identified with the *Religionism* which is to be distinguished from the inner essence or true significance of religion as 'a true law and guide for life.' Sri Aurobindo writes, "True religion is spiritual religion, that which seeks to live in the spirit, in what is beyond the intellect, beyond the aesthetic and ethical and practical being of man, and to inform and govern these members of our being by the higher light and laws of the spirit. *Religionism*, on the contrary, entrenches itself in some narrow pietistic exaltation of the lower members or lays exclusive stress on intellectual dogmas, forms and ceremonies, on some fixed and rigid moral code, on some religio-political or religio-social system."[21]

Sri Aurobindo thus observes that the spirituality is the inner essence of religion that can remove the defects of *Religionism* and guides a man to develop his potential divinity that can help him to realise truth through the establishment of unity or harmony in life and society. This harmonious development of life, in the observation of Sri Aurobindo, is the manifestation of perfection in man, expressed as the spirituality in religion. In the light of this prospect of transcendent religious consciousness by progressive transformation of one's mentality, Sri Aurobindo observes that different religions of the world are spread as it were, in different human situations from country to country, culture to culture, from age to age- as the evolution of the history of man, contain the different elements of truth as the expression of progressive perfection in man. Sri Aurobindo examines the contributions of different religions thus, "Each religion has helped mankind. Paganism increased in man the light of beauty, the largeness and height of his life, his aim at a many sided perfection; Christianity gave him some vision of divine love and charity; Buddhism has shown him a noble way to be wiser, gentler, purer; Judaism and Islam how to be religiously faithful in action and zealously devoted to God; Hinduism has opened to him largest and profoundest spiritual possibilities."[22] Evaluating the contributions of different religions in the growth of transcendent aspect and also in harmonious development

of human nature, Sri Aurobindo explains the transcendent integral consciousness of a transformed religious consciousness- where all religions had their roots, but each has to give up its restrictedness to proceed forward to an order beyond their rationalist or restricted intuitional attitudes, to rise to a transcendent condition which could be equally shared and enjoyed by the exponent of the different religions of the world as a scientist enjoys perfections of the different sciences in the emergent possibilities and possible perfections–not crying for a stop or for an ultimate. For Sri Aurobindo, "A religion which is itself a congeries of religions and which at the same time provides each man with its own turn of inner experience, would be the most in consonance with this purpose of Nature: it would be a rich nursery of spiritual growth and flowering, a vast multiform school of soul's discipline, endeavour, self-realisation."[23] This method of harmony, manifests the integral outlook or approach of the religion of Man, that develops the harmony in all religions; not for the elimination of minor differences or diversities, but for the transcendent consciousness revealed in each religion is experientially shared equally with respect by all developing religions of the world.

References

1. J. Ward, Naturalism and Agnosticism, Vol. II.
2. Karl Marx and Engles, on Religion.
3. Comte, A, General View of Positivism, translated by Bridges, J.H.
4. Sri Aurobindo, Religion–Aim and Nature, Religion, p. 1.
5. Sri Aurobindo, The Human Cycle, p. 191.
6. Sri Aurobindo, Heraclitus, p. 60.
7. Sri Aurobindo, The Future Evolution of Man, Edited by P.B. Saint-Hilaire, p. 23.
8. Lincoln Barnett, The Universe and Dr Einstein, p. 103.
9. Sir Julian Huxley, Evolution after Darwin, Vol. III. pp. 251-252.
10. R. N. Tagore, The Religion of Man, p. 10.
11. Sri Aurobindo, 'Religion–Aim and Nature', Religion, p. 1.
12. Bradley, F. H., Appearance and Reality, p. 388.
13. William James, Varieties of Religious Experience, p. 32.
14. S. Alexander, Space Time and Deity, Vol. II, p. 429.
15. S. K. Maitra, Sri Aurobindo Mandir Annual, Vol. II, p. 61.

16. Dr S. Radhakrishnan, Religion and Culture, p. 8.
17. Sri Aurobindo, The Human Cycle, p. 160.
18. Sri Aurobindo, The Life Divine, Vol. II, p. 696.
19. Sri Aurobindo, The Future Evolution of Man, p. 44.
20. *Ibid*, p. 45.
21. Sri Aurobindo, The Human Cycle, p. 220.
22. Sri Aurobindo and The Mother, on Religion, p. 15.
23. Sri Aurobindo, The Life Divine, Vol. II, p. 726.

Part - II

Importance of the Integral View of Sri Aurobindo in Cultivating Religion as the Realisation of Man, The Superhuman

The integral view of Sri Aurobindo is purely democratic as it recognises the contributions of different elements of the different religions of the world in the development of the true significance of the religion as the religion of Man; Sri Aurobindo's religion is spiritual in nature and is integral in its approach to life.

In the analysis of the integral outlook of the religion of Man, Sri Aurobindo explains religion as the expression of human nature and existence. Thus he, like Professor Toynbee and other historians, explains the importance of the human religion in the history of human life. In the history of life, Comte points out that religion contains the whole of human existence and Max Muller also emphasises that the true history of man is the history of religion. In this way, Sri Aurobindo, in the historical development of unity of human existence with his religion, puts an emphasis on the integrity of man, and religion as a broad humanist movement and transformation.

In the evaluation of the nature and the development of this integral consciousness–to Sri Aurobindo is a teleological and evolutionary progress of human life and religion, where human existence passes through the different stages through the expressions of different elements or qualities of life. These may lead to the expressions of different religions which can realise different qualities of life in different ways. In the evolution of this evolutionary progress, he, like the European Hegelians, puts an importance on reason in man and thus explains its significance in the evolution of religion; and then like American Pragmatists, he also accepts the value of religion in human life, but still unlike these thinkers, in broad intercultural context, he takes this process of evolution as the fulfillment of higher or wider purpose of life, and so abstract or restricted reason or particular element of life, according to Sri Aurobindo, is subordinated to the supra-rational element in life and evolution, towards an integral cosmic-psychic or psychic-cosmic experiences.

In this process of integral consciousness, Sri Aurobindo explains the significance of bodily and mental existence of man, where there will be the emergence of spiritual element in man as an integral process of body, mind and spirit, and religion ends with the expression of a transcendent and transforming spiritual or divine consciousness in experiential process and possibility. It is to be noted in this connection that the emergence of the transcendent spirituality in life is not a forcible elimination of particular element of life as expressed in particular religion, which, according to Bradley, may create a difference in life. But Sri Aurobindo thinks that the introduction of spirituality in an integral process of developing an integral consciousness recognising differences, which, according to him, is the accomplishment of life in *Yoga*. So this integral view of Sri Aurobindo's religion of Man, is the development of the transcendent spirituality or the divinity in human life, through a discipline of an integral process of *Yoga*. Thus, Sri Aurobindo writes, "Spiritual experience is the final aim and achievement of religion, its sky and sumit."[1]

This integral developmental process of the spiritual existence, Sri Aurobindo finally evaluates the nature of religion and the existence of man in an integral manner. This integral process unites man with religion as religion is the expression of the nature of man and man also stands on religion as the history of the progress of human life. This integral development of man and religion is the progress of the idea of Sri Aurobindo's religion of Man, is the advancement of human life and existence in different stages of the evolution of the nature of man as the evolution of his religion of life.

In the analysis of the different stages of evolution of life, Sri Aurobindo evaluates the nature and existence of man as spiritually perfect. This spirituality in man makes his material existence more significant as it does not ignore the materiality, but its end, on the other hand, is the divine change of man through the realisation of freedom from the limitation and contradiction of individuality or material *egoism* in a harmony as the spiritual freedom.

Thus, in the evaluation of human nature, Sri Aurobindo does not put any importance on the materialistic explanation of man, as a complex combination of matter or energy, or again the view of man, according to some sociologists, organicists, social psychologists, integrating man as the 'cell' of the society. But to Sri Aurobindo, all these explanations refer to the partial or one-sided approach to man. Man is something more than the combination of mere matter, energy or 'cell'. The creative personality of man, according to Sri Aurobindo, is for the fulfillment of some purpose, which, he observes, is not mere material, but is a conscious process of developing spirituality in man and society as the manifestation of divinity in individual and collective life. In this context, Sri Aurobindo writes, "....[*God*] having made man in His own image, with the ego as a centre of working, with the race, the collective Narayana, the Vishwamanava as the mould and circumscription, seeks to express in them some image of the unity, omniscience, omnipotence which are the self conception of the Divine."[2] This spiritual outlook of man as the expression of divinity in individual and collective life of man, eliminates one is restricted 'ego' which is responsible for creating conflicting situations and problems in society for "The exaltation of the collectivity, of the State, only substitutes the collective ego for the individual ego."[3] This 'ego' in human life creates different problems in mental, ethical and spiritual life and it also tries to solve these problems mechanically that may create a mechanical relation among men and it also is responsible for producing modern evils and evolutionary crisis in society. Sri Aurobindo evaluates thus, " Life, state, society, family, all surrounding powers seem to be in a league to lay their yoke on our spirit, compel us into their moulds, impose on us their mechanical interest and rough immediate convenience. We become parts of a machine; we are not, are hardly allowed to be in the true sense, manusya, purusa, souls, minds, free children of the spirit empower to develop the highest characteristic perfection of our being and make it our means of service to the race."[4] So, in a proper analysis of the development of man and society and their essential and intimate relation with each other, Sri Aurobindo emphasises the spirituality in life which removes the mechanical relation of man and society due to 'ego' but develops the universality in man through the presence of a divine integral consciousness in all. In this connection, it may be pointed out that Sri Aurobindo, unlike Hegelians and other ideologists, does not accept the submergence of an individual in the wider aggregation in society. In the analysis of his observation, it may be noted, "It is wrong to demand that the individual subordinates himself to the collectivity or merge in it, because it is by its most advanced individuals that the collectivity progresses and they can really advance only if they are free. But it is true that as the individual advances spiritually, he finds himself more and more united with the collectivity and the All."[5]

Thus, in the opinion of Sri Aurobindo, the spiritual development of the individual and collective life of man, solves the problems of life and society through the essential development of unity in all. Sri Aurobindo explains the three different streams of expressing this transcendent spiritual consciousness of human life: "These sway between the three principal preoccupations of our idealism, -the complete single development of the human being in himself, the perfectibility of the individual, a full development of the collective being, the perfectibility of society and more pragmatically restricted, the perfect or best possible relations of individual with individual and society and of community with community."[6] So, in this analysis of Sri Aurobindo, it is observed that the spiritual development of human life is the total development of man which refers to the individual and collective life of man through a development of an emergent integral consciousness present in man and society.

This, according to Sri Aurobindo, spirituality is the fundamental process as it includes both transcendental and experiential processes of life which is to be cultivated in man as the realisation of perfection in him and also is to be manifested in his collective existence through the development of perfect divinity in society. These realisation and manifestation of perfection or spirituality in life and society, in the opinion of Sri Aurobindo, is the expression of the true spiritual religion of Man. He observes, "True religion is spiritual religion that which seeks to live in the spirit, in what is beyond the intellect, beyond the aesthetic and ethical and practical being of man, and to inform and govern these members of ours being by the higher light and the law of the spirit."[7]

Thus, Sri Aurobindo observes that the development of the *spiritual religion* is the expression of the religion of Man which is to live '*in the spirit*', through the expression of his divine nature as the religion of life in his eternal existence in *contradictions into unity*. Sri Aurobindo writes, "It is true in a sense that religion should be the dominant thing in life, its light and law, but religion as it should be and is in its inner nature, its fundamental law of being, a seeking after God, the cult of spirituality, the opening of the deepest life of the soul to the indwelling God head, the eternal omnipresence."[8]

In connection with this analysis of the religion of Man as the expression of the spiritual nature or divine existence of man in and through the contradictions of life and society, Sri Aurobindo observes the unity of religion with life and also observes the essential expression of this unity as the unity in contradictions or diversities. It is spiritual or divine as it can reconcile the contradictions, overcoming all limitations through the development of divine unity in man and society. Thus, the proper object of the religion of Man is to express the divinity in his being or existence, which, according to Sri Aurobindo, "...is to discover the Infinite, the Absolute, the One, the Divine, who is all these things and yet no abstraction but a Being. Its work is a sincere living out of the true and intimate relations between man and God, relations of unity, relations of difference, relations of an illumined knowledge, an ecstatic love and delight, an absolute surrender and service, a casting of every part of our existence out of its normal status into an up rush of man towards the Divine and descent of the Divine into man."[9]

It may be noted thus that the religious life of man is the essential development of the divinity of his Being which is not the imposition of restrictions on this natural development of his life but fundamentally is an essential expression of the spirituality, potential in his existence. This idea of the religion of Man is to be evaluated by Sri Aurobindo, thus: "The religious life may be the first approach to the spiritual, but very often it is only a turning about in a round of rites, ceremonies and practices or set ideas and forms without any issue. The spiritual life, on the contrary, proceeds directly by a change of consciousness, a change from the ordinary consciousness, ignorant and separated from its true self and from God, to a greater consciousness in which one finds one's true being and comes first into direct and living contact and then into union with the Divine."[10]

So the development of the spirituality as the change of consciousness, for the realisation of the true being or divinity of man, is the final and fundamental idea of Sri Aurobindo's religion of Man which is the manifestation of inner potency or divine reality in the human existence and it is the emergence of new life or creative spirit other than his '*empirical ego*'. Dr Chatterjee rightly observes, "It should not be confused with intellectualism or idealism or ethicalism or religiosity - it is not a mental belief or creed or any kind of emotional aspiration. It means a total transformation of our whole being–a transformation which is due to the waking up of a 'new self' in us."[11] Its significance means a transformation of Man beyond Mental to Supramental order.

Thus, in the analysis of the proper meaning of Sri Aurobindo's idea of the religion of Man, it may be finally pointed out that its real significance lies in the spiritual transformation of the total being of man which is the '*inner change*' of man for the development of his outer life as the introduction of unity in the collective life of individuals. Here we may refer to the observation of Sri Aurobindo: "If humanity is to survive, a radical transformation of human nature is indispensible."[12]

True Significance of the Religion of Man as the Evolution of Man, The Superhuman, in the Individual Being

In the light of the proper evaluation of the idea of religion of Man as the eternal expression of universality or divinity in human existence, Sri Aurobindo also explains the significance of the religion of Man, the Universal as the *Superman or Superhuman*, in man, the individual and also explains the fundamental purpose or the object of the religion of Man as the eternal development and essential transformation of human nature from materiality to spirituality as the synthesis of material, mental, individual, social and spiritual existences of man for the expression of eternal unity and universality, in different states of life. 'Man', in this context of Sri Aurobindo's analysis, "is a spirit using the mind, life and body for an individual and a communal experience and self-manifestation in the universe."[13]

So the 'self-manifestation', according to Sri Aurobindo, is the expression of the spirit of universality, immanent in man and also is a unity with Absolute or Transcendent idea of Universality, which is to be manifested in the different stages of life as the expression of diversity in different degrees. Men have to work and the whole process of spirituality, religion and divinity by saying that when one can go beyond the material levels to the supramental processes, then by a transformation in that order, one can realise spirituality in all.

In the background of this analysis of the divine existence of man, Sri Aurobindo evaluates the significance of human life in a more creative manner, where his existence is not taken as the shadow or mere appearance of divinity, nor taken as something existing without divinity.

This limited approach or separative tendency, emphasises the particular aspect of man or the materiality of human existence, creating '*ego*' in man, that, in the observation of Sri Aurobindo in '*The Life Divine*', is due to 'original ignorance', responsible for producing contradictions or evils in life and society. So why as a Man is restricted to his bodily mental processes and not lifted to the Supramental Order by a total transformation, one is still below the spiritual order.

Though this '*ego*' in material life is a practical or pragmatic aspect of individual, still its significance lies not in the contradictions or isolations but in the reconciliation, as the expression of unity as the potential divinity or universality in man. So, in the background of this divinity, all the diversities or differences become real as the significance of this reality lies in the development of unity in different stages through which man can overcome or transcend the contradictions or disunities of life. Sri Aurobindo writes, "The individual therefore exists though he exceeds the little separative ego; the universal exists and is embraced by him but it does not absorb and abolish all individual differentiation, even though by his universalising himself, the limitation which we call the ego is overcome."[14]

This process of developing universality, overcoming contradictions, as the expressions of Transcendent Divine in the different stages of human life, finally reveals the eternal relation of divine unity in love, potent in man as immanent godness or divinity in human existence.

Thus, in this analysis of human existence, Sri Aurobindo significantly evaluates the human nature as the expression of universal or divine nature of man as his proper religion of life that makes the material existence of man real, through the reconciliation of the contradictions of material life in unity, revealing divinity in different stages as the expressions of the 'divinity of man'. This manifestation of divinity in different states of life and society, is possible through the expression of the divine quality of love, potent in man, which is also manifested through the different human relations, introducing unity as the '*humanity of God*'.

Thus, the idea of the religion of Man, as introduced by Sri Aurobindo, is the eternal expression of divinity in man that establishes the universal or divine outlook as God in man and man in God. This idea of divinity and the process of developing this idea of divine unity in human life, according to Sri Aurobindo, are spiritual; where he observes, "The Individual is a centre of the whole Universal Consciousness"[15]. This spiritual process of developing 'Universal Consciousness' as divine unity in man, accepts the reality of individual being as the centre of the concentration of the consciousness for the purposive manifestation of his potential divinity in different stages of life.

In this process, Sri Aurobindo observes, consciousness works through the concentration and the expansion; universe is the expansion of Absolute consciousness in infinite space and time and the individual is the concentration of infinite consciousness within spatio-temporal limits. Both individual and world seek the divinity as the seat of Absolute consciousness or God and thus the nature or world seeks divinity and God also is manifested in nature or universe in different stages. Similarly the individual man, being potentially Divine or Universal, gradually develops divinity or universality in his life in different degrees through the realisation of oneness or unity in man, world and God. In this process of developing unity or universality, the individuality or '*ego*' of man as his finiteness or limitation, gradually merged in Infinite as the deepest or highest unity where individual also is an ontological reality, existent in and through the divinity.

It may be observed thus that the individual man, being an ontological reality, develops universality through the realisation of divine value of unity of finiteness and infiniteness, individuality and transcendentality. Again God or Ultimate Reality as the substratum of the divine value of unity, also manifests Himself in different states of life and existence. This interpretation of Sri Aurobindo, in the background of the idea of *Upanishad,* is the manifestation or evolution of unity or whole, through the different parts or stages of human life and world towards unity or completeness where the individuality is never be existent without universality as this idea of universality is the accomplishment of individuality in unity.

In the context of this analysis, though Sri Aurobindo, like all other Absolutists, observes, "...The particular, the individual can have no self-existence, no truth, no valid force except in so far as it reflects rightly and relates and confirms itself justly to the universal, to the all-being, the all-knowledge, the all-will...", still he states further that "...the universal also has no self-existence, truth or validity except as it expresses the divine Being, Knowledge, Will, Power, Delight of Him who surpasses all Universe, so much so that with a petty fragment of His being and a single ray of His consciousness He has created all these world."[16] In the analysis of the unity of the individuality and the universality in this manner, Sri Aurobindo develops the idea of reality as whole, where he, like Bradley, accepts universal is individual, and again in the background of *Vedanta,* he also observes that self or universality is equally real and true individual. Though McTaggart refers to the difficulty of intellect, as mind cannot grasp this idea, still the possibility of this wholeness refers to the completeness of man where he is taken as the cosmic individual, who gradually becomes complete through the manifestation of potent universality, in different stages, transcending the limitations of those stages, through the realisation of unity of individuality and transcendentality. This process of developing unity or universality transfers the nature of man, the individual, to Man, the Universal, and makes the evolution of Universal Man in individual man, possible; and thus makes the evolution of the Universality in the different states of the individual and the collective or social life of man, real.

Thus, the process of evolution of man as the transformation of human nature, explains the significance of the human existence in an integral form, which is a synthesis of materiality, sociality and spirituality. In a long process of evolution of matter and life, the human organism is evolved, which asserts his material existence in this material world and then after the evolution of his material existence with its relations with other human organism, the social existence of man is asserted which is the evolution of unity in society. But the evolution of this material and social existences of man lead to the development of the freedom in unity as the expression of his potential perfection or universal or divine nature which is evaluated by Tagore, "...Man appeared and turned the course of this evolution from an indefinite march of physical aggrandizement to a freedom of a more subtle perfection. This has made possible his progress to become unlimited and has enabled him to realise the boundless in his power."[17] The realisation of this boundless power is the accomplishment of universality and also is the manifestation of this Universal Reality or Absolute in different stages of life towards unity in its diversities or differences, which, in the opinion of Sri Aurobindo, is purely spiritual as the expression of Supreme or Absolute Consciousness. So, evolution, according to Sri Aurobindo, is a teleological expression of Consciousness, which is veiled in matter and fights for its expression in the life of animal in a rudimentary form and finally expressed in human life in a more organised form where we get the synthesis of matter, life and mind. Human body is a form of inconscient matter that expresses his animality or low form of life, but his mind also expresses the higher form of reason that inspires him to transcend the inconsistencies of material existence and thus reveals the significance of human existence. In the evolution of his inner states of mind, revealing the highest form of divine unity as the synthesis of individuality and transcendentality.

So evolution, in the opinion of Sri Aurobindo, has the outward or the visible aspect of matter in the bodily existence and also has inward or invisible aspect of mind in the development of unity or universality as the highest form of consciousness in man. Thus, in the process of evolution as the process of transformation of Consciousness, Sri Aurobindo observes firstly its existence in involution as the potential containment of life in matter and potentiality of mind or consciousness in life and unity of matter and mind or consciousness in man. Thus, Sri Aurobindo thinks that a gradual ascent of matter into life and life into consciousness becomes possible due to prior descent or involution of Absolute Consciousness in life and matter. So the involution of consciousness in different states leads to the evolution as its expression in different stages: (a) matter (*jada*), (b) life (*prana*), (c) psyche (*chaitanya-purusa*), (d) mind (*manasa*), (e) supermind (*vijnana or Rita-chit*), and (f) existence (*sat*).

Evolution, in this manner, is not a mere change in a mechanical process or is not an effect of chance variation. Darwin points out that, evolution proceeds under the guidance of three principles: e.g., struggle for existence, survival of the fittest and adaptation to environment. The teleological and integral or comprehensive view of Sri Aurobindo suggests that the evolution is guided by 'the will to know', 'the will to grow', and 'the will to perfection' through the creative processes of widening as the expansion of the field of operation involving the ascent as the progress in different stages, implying integration that leads to the development of unity in different stages, expressing the infiniteness of Highest Being in the integral existence of man.

Thus, man acquires a unique position in evolution, because a man as a synthesis of matter and mind makes the transformation of unconscious to conscious stage possible which gradually urges him to realise his own existence as self-consciousness that finally leads to the realisation of the Absolute Consciousness as the highest state of divine unity. So the meaning of evolution is the change of consciousness that makes the higher possibility of becoming and transforms the Nature and man integrally. In the pre-human stage, consciousness was not adequate, as evolution went into mere bodily changes, but in the post-human stages the evolution proceeds with the change of consciousness, that, in the observation of Sri Aurobindo, is spiritually significant. Sri Aurobindo explains the significance of the spirituality thus: "Spirituality is a progressive awakening to the inner reality of our being, to a spirit, soul which is other than our mind, life and body. It is an inner aspiration to know, to enter into contact and union with the greater Reality beyond, which also pervades the universe and dwells in us, and, as a result of that aspiration, that contact and that union, a turning, a conversion, a birth into a new being."[18]

Evaluating the significance of spirituality in evolution of man in this way, Sri Aurobindo points out that as man with his technical knowledge, may help Nature to produce new types of animal and plants, so he also may help Nature for the transformation of his own nature for the emergence of spirituality and thus he will realise the existence of Supramental Consciousness in him and in Nature that will finally help him to realise to deeper relatedness or unity in him and Nature. This progress, according to Sri Aurobindo, is a spiritual progress as the progress of soul in man, which is the synthesis of one's, material or bodily and mental and transcending orders-going beyond the mental order is the development of the human existence which according to Sri Aurobindo, is possible through his psychical development and transformation for the new state of the *'Supramental instrumentation of Nature'*.

In the analysis of the psychical development as the progress of the psychic being of man, Sri Aurobindo observes its significance in human personality that is veiled in the human body, life and mind and eternally evolved and gradually developed in different states and it has no destruction at the time of death when mental, vital and physical beings are destroyed. So psychic being of man in the form of individual self thus continues to exist through ages and passes from life to life and works in cosmic evolution. It is not to be confused with vital principle or vital being that guides life, the activities of life like passions, desires, emotions, etc. as a real individual self, it also is not also to be confused with 'ego', which is mentally oriented in producing limitations, separations, contradictions or evils, which are to be removed through the gradual transformation in the order of supramental and psychic being.

The development of psychic being, according to Sri Aurobindo, is due to the supramental progress of human life through a radical change and integral transformation of Nature to the stage of mind. It is for the evolution of supramental being in man as the proper guide of Nature and Mind, and finally a unity between mind and to the order of supermind is to be established when mind will ascend to supermind and supermind will descend to mind. In this reciprocal–ascent–descent process, the human existence gets fullest development. In the observation of Sri Aurobindo, it may be said, "...there must take place as the crowning movement the ascent in to the supermind and the transforming descent of the supramental consciousness into our entire being and nature." The transformation of human being and human nature, according to Sri Aurobindo, is the 'Triple transformation' of man in the orders from the Mind to the Superior Order–where Psychic, Spiritual and Supramental Transformations form a totality in a dynamic sense of reciprocity.

Psychic being, which is veiled in individual existence, proceeds towards supramental stage through its gradual revelation. The psychic being as spiritual staff or real self in man, through an integral process of the triple path ways of knowledge, devotion and action, gradually withdraws itself from the lower orders- outer to the inner, and thus becomes the inner Person or *Purusa.* This *Purusa* represents the True Being for the realisation of One or Divine Being as continually fluent and dynamic. In this context, it may be noted that Sri Aurobindo, though apparently follows the Sankhya doctrine of a distinction between *Purusa* or Conscious Being and *Prakriti* or Nature, still he transcends the dualism by indicating their basic continuity as recognised by Sankhya, through the development of infiniteness as divine unity of consciousness and Nature through a proper controlling of body, mind and soul–*Yoga* and *Tantra.*

In this way the second stage of spiritual transformation becomes possible, overcoming all divisions, separations or finiteness. In this way, man can transcend all limitations or finiteness through the development of divinity as the realisation of divine values, like Truth, Beauty and Goodness, and God, as the substratum of these infinite values, appears as human and real through His manifestation in the infinite existence of man. This is an ascent to and or not realised by any apparently present world.

In this process of manifestation and the transformation of finite to infinity, the ignorance or false knowledge about the division of the finite and the infinite, is removed through the process of supramental transformation that is the Truth consciousness or Self-awareness as Divine Unity, which is permanent and effective.

In this process of supramental transformation, the finite mind can rise to the Supermind through the following stages e.g.,

1. Leading to Higher Mind is a clear, spiritual or conceptual knowledge about which Sri Aurobindo observes, "An all awareness emerging from the original identity carrying the truths, the identity held in itself, conceiving swiftly, victoriously, multitudinously, formulating and by self-power of the idea effectually realising its conceptions, is the character of this greater mind of knowledge."[19]
2. Illumined Mind is the spiritual light of inner power: "As the Higher Mind brings a greater consciousness into the being through the spiritual idea and its power of truth, so the Illumined Mind brings in a still greater consciousness through a Truth-sight and Truth-light and its seeing and seizing power."[20]
3. Then there is a further ascent to Intuitive Mind through intuition that transforms the life and body and changes consciousness into will, feelings and emotions and thus develops the knowledge of identity to an intuitive order. According to Sri Aurobindo, "Intuition is a power of consciousness nearer and more intimate to the original knowledge by identity; for it is something that leaps out direct from a concealed identity."[21] Through this intuitive knowledge, mind acquires the powers

of seeing, hearing, touching truth and thus proceeds to an order of spontaneous relation of truth and truth. This mental process is thus ascent aspects. The descent from the highest order to other basic orders from the overmind to the merely mental order is a provision or Descent.

4. Over-mind is the proper descent of Supermind as the power of cosmic consciousness, completely eliminates separateness, finiteness or 'ego', establishes a harmony and embraces totality. Sri Aurobindo points out, "What to the mental reason are irreconcilable differences present themselves to the Over-mind intelligence as co-existent correlatives; what to the mental reason are contraries are to the Over-mind intelligence complementaries."[22] Thus, all combinations, co-relations are possible here for the proper manifestation of Divinity, where feeling, thought and emotion become cosmic, all embracing, spiritual and infinite.

But it should be noted here that Over-mind cannot transform the entire Nature or Inconscience, for this the supramental transformation as a radical change or transfiguration through the intervention or direct influence of supramental power on human existence, is necessary.

Thus, in the evaluation of these different stages, it may be said that these are the manifestations of Reality in different grades in different degrees in and through the transformation of conscient to the Superconscient and the change of matter, life, and different stages of mind to supermind which also are taken as the expression of Reality in the different stages of spiritual evolution.

In the analysis of the spiritual evolution as the realisations of Reality in different stages of human life and the manifestations of Reality in different degrees, it may be pointed out that evolution starts with involution of Reality or *Saccidananda* in matter and gradually there is the appearance of Existence, Consciousness and Bliss in different higher forms, which, in the emergence of man are synthesised in a highest form for the evolution of physical, vital and mental man as the different stages of Nature towards the development of spiritual man. In the evolution of the spiritual man, we find the synthesis of humanity and divinity, where Nature ascends through the conscious process of human mind and extends his existence in the material world towards psychic self and God, which is nothing but the extension of human mind or heart for the realisation of highest state of the divine value of perfection or unity in man, world and God, transcending his limitation or finiteness.

It may be noted here that Sri Aurobindo's idea of the evolution of man as the extension of his psychic being, is not merely an ascent but also the transformation of human nature and 'Psychisation', which in the observation of Sri Aurobindo, "means the change of the lower nature bringing right vision into the mind, right impulse and feeling into the vital, right movement and habit into the psychical all turned towards the Divine, all based on love, adoration, bhakti, finally the vision and sense of the mother everywhere, in all as well as in the heart, here force working in the being etc., faith, consecration, surrender."[23] Thus, in the development of psychic being as true-self or real individual man, there will be the realisation of divine value, through different methods of accomplishment, for the complete or supramental transformation or for the descent of supermind in the highest form of appearance of '*Superman*' or '*Superhuman*', the Universal or Absolute, in man, the individual. The development of this supramental being in individual existence is to introduce unity of individuality with universality, expressed in human thoughts and activities that manifest the harmony of humanity and divinity: "The supramental being will realise the harmony of his individual self with the cosmic self, of his individual will and action with the cosmic Will and Action,"[24] for the inauguration of the Universality or Infiniteness in the finite individual.

References

1. Sri Aurobindo, The Life Divine, Vol. II, p. 692.
2. Sri Aurobindo, The Life Divine, Vol. I, p. 18.
3. Sri Aurobindo, The Future Evolution of Man, p. 53.
4. Sri Aurobindo, Essays on the Geeta, Calcutta, 1942, Vol. II, p. 337.
5. Sri Aurobindo, The Future Evolution of Man, pp. 49-50.
6. *Ibid*, p. 48.
7. Sri Aurobindo and The Mother, On Religion, pp. 20-21.
8. *Ibid*, p. 20.
9. *Ibid*, p. 13.

10. *Ibid*, p. 19.
11. Dr P B Chatterjee, Towards *Supermanhood*: The Philosophy of Sri Aurobindo, p. 42.
12. Sri Aurobindo, The Future Evolution of Man, p. 54.
13. Sri Aurobindo, The Synthesis of *Yoga*, p. 713.
14. The Life Divine, Vol. II, pp. 92-93.
15. *Ibid*, Vol. I, p. 45.
16. Ideal and Progress, pp. 16-17.
17. R. N. Tagore, The Religion of Man, p. 10.
18. The Future Evolution of Man, p. 68.
19. The Life Divine, Vol. II, p. 788.
20. The Life Divine, Vol. I, p. 334.
21. *Ibid*, Vol. II, p. 946.
22. The Life Divine, Vol. II, p. 330.
23. Sri Aurobindo Mandir Annual, No. 6, August 1947, p. 41.
24. The Gnostic Being, The Future Evolution of Man, p. 113.

Part - III

The Divine Life on Earth and the Ways for Attaining the State of Human Freedom

A careful examination of Sri Aurobindo's idea of the religion of Man finally evaluates the evolution of *Superman as Superhuman* in the individual that is a teleological manifestation of the universality in the finite being. The development of this universality or infiniteness is the expression of total man which is the realisation of the final end of human existence. Sri Aurobindo observes that 'To be and to be fully' is the summum bonum of man and Nature. 'To be fully' is an integral awareness of the whole being in one's own self as the development of intrinsic and integral force of one's being that is to have the full delight of being which is the realisation of the hidden existence, consciousness and bliss. This means that to become full is to become universal as all is one and to be universally is to be transcendentally also.[1]

This idea of Sri Aurobindo explains the total nature of man as the unity of individuality and universality that recognises the material existence of man as the explanation of physical, vital and mental states and then there will be a reconciliation of all these levels of existence through a process of transcendence of these stages in an accomplishment of highest state of unity as the emergence of the fullness of Super conscience in all states of life.

This process of transcending materiality and developing unity of materiality and transcendentality in man, according to Sri Aurobindo, is an inauguration of the divinity of man which is nothing but the spiritual progress or transformation of the basic human nature. He writes thus: "Spirituality is in its essence an awakening to the inner reality of our being, to a spirit, self, or soul which is other than our mind, life and body, an inner aspiration to know, to feel, and to be. That to enter into contact with the greater Reality beyond and pervading the universe which inhabits our own being also, to be in communion with It and union with It, and a turning, a conversion, a transformation of our whole being as a result of the aspiration, the contact, the union, a growth or waking into a new nature." This is the development of totality in human existence, a sense of a completeness or fullness in man, which, according to Sri Aurobindo, is not merely the manifestation of universal spirit but is also a radical and integral transformation of human nature through the emergence of *Superman as Superhuman* in human existence.

The *Superman as Superhuman* is always present only it has to be discovered by a progressive detachment from the attachment for the lower orders. *Superman as Superhuman* transcends different stages of life and mind of man and this supramental state in human existence, like the idea of Deity in Alexander's philosophy, is unknowable to mind till actually the emergent duality arises, but to Sri Aurobindo it was already in Nature, only not discovered but can be realised in one's life through an intervention of Superconsciousness is also a requisite. So the transition from mind to supermind or intellectual to spiritual level is an evolutionary progress of Nature to Supernature and this is also a natural process and cannot be excluded. So one has to posit a descent of Superconsciousness in Man, as the highest qualitative expression of Nature in Evolution.

The descent of Superconscience in man and the ascent of man in different stages towards this supreme state, are the manifestations of Reality or truth consciousness in different degrees and these realisations of reality in different stages in different degrees, according to Sri Aurobindo, help a man to be free from the limitation or determinism of Nature and thus in the final state of existence, a man realises his highest state of freedom in unity when an individual man becomes *Superman or Superhuman* as the Universal and the Infinite through the inauguration of God in him as the 'divinity of man', and

God or Ultimate Reality also descends in man as the 'humanity of God'. These creative ideas of 'divinity' and 'humanity', expressed through the highest state of human freedom, is evaluated by N Pearson, ".....to become fully conscious of the Divine and to recognise Him in all appearances and statuses, and in all conditions, is the one effective way of knowing and growing into that all-encompassing Consciousness."[2] Truly speaking Sri Aurobindo does not foster one-way extensive consciousness.

Thus, it may be pointed out that the inauguration of unity through the emergence of *Superman as Superhuman* in the supermind of man, according to Sri Aurobindo, is the 'Real-Idea' or Truth Consciousness in man as the unity of individuality and Universality towards the manifestation of his universal nature in the different stages of human existence. Professor Maitra explains this state thus: "The Supermind thus is the creative idea which retains to the full the truth of the Supreme Reality. Mind, Life and Matter are an inferior expression of it which serves as a goal towards which these are trying to move."[3] This may be treated as the supreme or final state of human existence, where all movements of life become full and complete.

This completeness or fullness of human life and existence in the state of Supermind, according to Professor Maitra, is ".....nothing else than God as Lord and Creator. It is, however, different from the Ishvara of the *Vendantist* or the Demiurge of Plato."[4] As *Ishvara* of *Vedanta* is conditioned or limited by *Maya*, and Demiurge as the idea of the creator of Plato is conditioned by the concept of 'archetype' out of which he creates the world, and even the Absolute Reality of Hegel as all in all, is also conditioned by Will, are thus different from Sri Aurobindo's idea of the highest state of Reality in man as *Superman or Superhuman*, which is a gradual evolution of the potential divinity of human nature that ascends through the different stages towards the realisation of the supreme state of divinity, and thus finally Divine Spirit also descends through the Supermind as the highest state of human existence.

The descent of the Supermind on man makes the human life more significant through the development of creative personality, expressing the potential universality in his material existence through the transcendence of contradiction or limitation as finiteness for the emergence of infiniteness as its highest reconciliation of contradictions. This development of infinite personality as the transformation of being, according to some thinkers, is purely human, which is the highest form of the development of divinity in human existence. Dr Rao points out, "The Supermind is not the personal God of the theist. It is Divine Will. Its descent alone can transform human existence into divine glory. Man has to stand aside and willingly make room for the descent of the supermind."[5]

Expression of divinity in the final state of the supermind in man, develops a highest state of unity which is free from all conditions or limitations. It is the final state of human freedom as it is not the imposition of something on man, but is the highest state of extension of different stages of life where there will be the reconciliation of all stages into an integral potentiality. In the development of this supreme state of integral existence, Sri Aurobindo, in 'The Life Divine', explains the three states of Supermind: 'The first finds the inalienable unity of things, the second modifies that unity so as to support the manifestation of the Many in One and One in Many; the third further modifies it so as to support the evolution of a diversified individuality which, by the action of Ignorance, becomes in us at a lower level, the illusion of the separate ego." These contributions of supermind in the development of an integral consciousness in human life and existence, have the significance in three stages: firstly, it is the *Saccidananda* in space and time that is an immanent aspect of unity as Existence, Consciousness and Bliss. Secondly, there is an appearance of plurality with a potential unity that is expressed through many and finally unites them in One. Thirdly, the expression of plurality in different individual state of existence in the diversities of the material world finally proceed through the different stages for their reconciliation in unity in the highest state of supermind. In 'The Life Divine', Sri Aurobindo writes, "Thus the elements of division have come into being. Firstly, the infinity of the One has translated itself into an extension in conceptual Time and Space; Secondly, the omnipresence of the One in that self-conscious extension translates itself into a multiplicity of the conscious soul, the many Purusas of the Sankhya; Thirdly, the multiplicity of soul-forms has translated itself into a divided habitation of the extended unity."

So progressive integration as a process and as a final state of existence, is naturally evolved in human life as its potential nature through a natural way of union or *Yoga*, which, on the one hand, is the realisation of unity as an end, through the different stages of life and on the other hand, is the application of unity as a means, through the creative process of life. In this background, Sri Aurobindo evaluates, natural and integral process of *Yoga* or union which is "….a methodized effort towards self-perfection by the expression of the potentialities latent in the being and a union of individual with the universal and transcendent Existence, we see partially expressed in man and in the cosmos."[6]

In this process of analysis of life and existence of man as 'a union of individual with the universal', it is observed that the being of a man is a perfect state of union or *Yoga* which unites him with the state of universality as the expression of the divine unity, potential in him and thus his universal or divine nature, expressed through the different states of unity and interrelationship, finally reveals the supreme states of life as the unity of the humanity and the divinity. Thus, *Yoga*, as a method of realising the proper essence of man is also the expression of his highest aim as the divine union or *Yoga*, which, in the opinion of Keshavmurti: "In essence the man and his Maker are One, but in the universal play they become separated, as it were, and the longing for reunion, for liberation from separation, is that which sets the course of *Yoga*."[7]

In the background of this evaluation, *Yoga* has both epistemological and ontological considerations as *Yoga* is both end and means or method; but finally this difference or distinction is culminated in the idea of being as unity where all explanations or evaluations of philosophy and religion are finally assimilated in union as *Yoga*; which, according to Sri Aurobindo, is the realisation of integral Divine as "nothing but practical psychology."[8] It is because the evolution of life as religion and the evolution of knowledge as philosophy must follow the method of *Yoga*, as evolution seeks Divine in the process of *Yoga* or Union as integrality of humanity and divinity, in the highest state of being. In the development of this integral outlook of *Yoga*, Sri Aurobindo also explains all other approaches to life and existence as Yogic disciplines, like,

(a) *Hatha Yoga* is a psycho-physical system that uses the physical and vital workings in human organism for opening the door of higher consciousness through different postural exercises like *asanas, pranayama,* etc.

(b) *Raja Yoga* is a psychological progress for the freedom of mental being in human body. This method or discipline contains *Yamas*, regulations of moral control over desires, passions, due to egoism, *Niyamas*, directions for peace and calmness as the preparations for the concentration on divinity in the state of *Samadhi* through *asanas* and *pranayama.*

(c) Three ways of *Jnana Yoga*, *Bhakti Yoga* and *Karma Yoga.*

(i) *Jnana Yoga* is a method of examination, *vicara* and the knowledge of difference, *viveka*, of phenomenal nature of being, *Prakriti*, as distinguished from pure consciousness or self as *Purusa* who makes the significance of Union or *Yoga*, complete through the inauguration of divinity in human existence.

(ii) *Bhakti Yoga* is a method of developing the emotional quality of human love that directs a man to love God as Supreme Person as the substratum of all qualities or values. Traditional *Bhakti Yoga* contains worship and meditation; the former leads to the adoration of God as beloved and thus in the later form there will be a development of intimacy of God as lover and man as beloved that finally develops unity of man and God.

(iii) *Karma Yoga* is the process of developing individual will to be merged with the Divine Will through different moral activities, expressing the spirit of detachment through different disinterested duties and service for others. The cultivation of this spirit in man, helps a man to be free from limitations or contradictions, due to narrow or self-interest and thus can realise the greater self in him as the unity of individuality and universality, revealing Divine Will.

In this analysis of these traditional *Yoga*s, it is observed that the fundamental end of all these methods, is to realise unity as divinity in life and existence. But their approaches to unity are one sided and partial. *Hatha Yoga* works on gross body, *Raja Yoga* acts on subtle body and other methods of realising unity, introduced by other processes are either the way of *Jnana*, or of *Bhakti* or of *Karma*, cultivating the particular quality like knowledge or love or work, the fundamental concern of which is not with this world as it is taken as a continuous state of ignorance.

But the fundamental object of Sri Aurobindo's idea of the religion of Man is not to negate the earth or earthly existence of man as ignorance or illusion or *maya*, but to accept and to develop the significance of the worldly existence of man as his self-fulfillment in this world through the introduction of an integral experience as an end, in and through the interrelated process formulating an *Integral Yoga*. The final end of this process of *Yoga*, is to introduce the divine life on earth through the transformation of lower nature to the Divine Nature, when there will be the change of man to *Superman as Superhuman* through the development of integrated personality as the totality of individuality and universality.

For this integral or overall development, the *Integral Yoga* is a process of recognising all the contributions of different *Yoga*s. Sri Aurobindo observes that all forms of *Yoga*s are psychological methods for perfection, emphasising this or that particular aspect of man; but integral psychology prefers the integral development of all aspects of man and thus all these one-sided approaches are perfected through a total development in the process of *Integral Yoga*. In this context, *Integral Yoga, Integral Psychology* and *Integral Philosophy* are closely related with one another.

In this emphatic or a culminating process, Sri Aurobindo's idea of *Integral Yoga* tries to transform the nature of man from his *ego* to real self and thus develops his total being as the *Integral Absolute*, where there is the possibility of expressing the highest freedom in unity in and through different individual variations in material world. This type of the integral realisation of truth consciousness in plurality, expresses the integral view of freedom and integral nature of Reality, revealed through the integral perfection of humanity. For the development of this state of perfection, Sri Aurobindo puts an equal importance on different aspects of knowledge, devotion and works, emphasised in different *Yogas*, but in the integral process, all these aspects of man as the expressions of particular aspects of truth are to be harmonised in love, as '*Love*', according to Sri Aurobindo, 'is the crown of works and the flowering of knowledge'. This human method of love, as the human approach to Reality, expressing harmony in all aspects of man, revealing the totality of human nature that finally manifests the perfect state of Truth or Reality as unity of man and God as the transformation of human mind as Supermind and man to *Superman or Superhuman*. This integral development of man, in this integral process, is evaluated by Sri Aurobindo, in 'The Synthesis of *Yoga*': "In the *Integral Yoga* these three lines of approach give up their exclusions, meet and coalesce or spring out of each other; liberated from the mind's veil over the self, we live in the Transcendence, enter by the adoration of the heart into the oneness of a supreme love and bliss, and all our forces of being uplifted into the one Force, our will and works surrendered into one Will and Power, assume the dynamic perfection of the Divine Nature."

In the background of the analysis of the human existence and its advancement, it may thus be observed that the total development of man is a process of Integration through a triple transformation - psychic, spiritual and supramental that, is not complete at the mere vital and mental stages of human existence. For this, the opening of the inner being or the inner psychic being is required and for the stable and permanent transformation, the supramental change as the ascent of mind into Supermind (Spirit) and the descent of supramental consciousness into the whole being and nature (to the stage of Matter), is fundamentally necessary.

This change or progress of human life in the integral process, is gradual, that, according to Sri Aurobindo, requires the unitive activities of the instruments of *sastra, utsaha, guru* and *kala* and this integral change thus expresses the different stages of union or *Yoga* as the manifestation of divinity which is the radical change of the whole being of man and this changed humanity as the basis of divine life on earth, becomes creative through the unity of materiality and sociality, individuality and universality, when there will be the rising from mind to Supermind, man to *Superman or Superhuman*, through the creative development of his Gnostic Being, which, according to Sri Aurobindo, '...will be the perfect consummation of the spiritual man', who '...will realise the harmony of his individual self with the cosmic self, of his individual will and action with the cosmic Will and Action' that reveals 'The Law of the Supermind' which '...is unity fulfilled in diversity.'[9]

The overall development of the creative personality of man as the development Gnostic Being, is not supernatural or not the appearance of Nietschein *Superman*, but it is the development of universal spirit in the individual existence when he will be free from the limitation of the separative individuality but will enjoy freedom in totality in all as the extension of his own being in everything. This state of realisation is the accomplishment of the highest state of unity or oneness as the expression of the divinity, which is '...of the self by the self and in the self.'[10] When the Gnostic Being will live as Divine Being for the Divine when it will be a perfect instrument for this manifestation of divine values as the expression of the Supernature of divinity. Thus, the being of man as Gnostic Being finally expresses the highest state of the divinity of Man and in this state there will be the expression of God or Divine, through the manifestation of humanity as divine value of *Ananda* or perfect Bliss in life and society.

In the analysis of this highest state of human existence as in freedom in unity, some are of opinion that, separation of *ego* in the individual, loses its identity and merges in universality and thus, the individuality of man is lost and so the question about the survival of the individual personality does not arise. Again others are of opinion, that the individual is not lost in Universal, but is reformed or developed and this reformation or development is the replacement of individual ego by Universal Spiritual Man. But in the observation of Sri Aurobindo, from the integral point of view, the distinction of individuality and universality as personality and impersonality does not arise at all, as he points out that these are the inseparable aspects of one Reality and thus he states that, ".....there is very clearly no opposition, no incompatibility, no impossibility of a co-existence or one existence of the Impersonal and the Person; they are each other, live in one another, melt into each other, and yet in a way can appear as if different ends, sides, obverse and reverse of the same Reality." So, in the light of this observation, it may be said that Gnostic individual is a person who expresses significantly the highest or divine value of infiniteness or universality and thus makes the divinity of man as the manifestation of God in man, possible. In the context of this idea of Sri Aurobindo, it may be expressed through his words, "The mental man that we are changed into the Gnostic soul, the truth-conscious godhead, the Vijnanmaya purusha"[11]

Thus, Gnostic Person or *Vijnanmaya Purusha*, is a complete and harmonised personality, revealed through the individual, material, social and spiritual states of human existence in their transforming processes in evolution.

Generally, material or individual existence of man, is in conflict with others, due to the conflict of individual and social interests. This is responsible for producing moral and social contradiction or evils. But in the development of Gnostic or harmonised personality, all this conflicts or contradictions are removed through the development of total being of man when the questions of ethical and social problems do not arise at all, because all these problems, due to disharmony, disunity are finally reconciled through the introduction of freedom in integral consciousness. In this context, the opinions of Kant and Bradley, may be referred to as these thinkers observes that ethical man is always in a conflict and if this conflict is removed, the problems of ethics becomes redundant. So in the development of Gnostic personality, the Gnostic evolution of man becomes complete when an individual is free from all conceptual limitations or contradictions through a realisation of perfection in the harmonised development of his physical, vital and mental being. In the observation of Sri Aurobindo, it may be pointed out, "Health, strength, duration, godly happiness and ease, liberation from suffering, are a part of the physical perfection which the Gnostic evolution is called upon to realise."[12]

This physical perfection of man leads to the perfection of his social existence which removes the conflict between individuality and sociality through the introduction of harmony in the human life and society. This harmony, as a moral or social law is not imposed from the outside, but it is a self-imposed law that follows from the inherent order of completeness or *Svadharma* of his own nature or *Svabhava*. So in the development of Gnostic personality there is no conflict between freedom in unity in social being and necessity of following the law of harmony; because Gnostic Person voluntarily or willingly manifests his nature as the expression of this law that expresses unity in individual and social life as the manifestation of Oneness as Universal Truth. Sri Aurobindo thus observes, "The Gnostic life will reconcile freedom and order. There will be an entire accord between the free expression of the individual and his obedience to the inherent law of the supreme and universal Truth of things."[13]

The expression of Unity as Universal Truth in individual and social being as the expression of inherent nature of Gnostic Person as the law of harmony, leads to the expression of spiritual life which is the unity of material, social and transcendental aspects of life into unity that finally manifests the proper religion of Man as the expression of total, self-fulfilled and complete Man, revealing the highest state of freedom in unity of divinity and humanity as the unity of God and man in the Gnostic Being, developing the possibility of the divine life on earth. In order to explain this process, Sri Aurobindo firmly states that, "The transcendent aspect of the spiritual life is indispensible for the freedom of the spirit; but it will harmonise it an unshakable foundation. For the Gnostic being, to act in the world does not signify a lapse from unity..."[14]

In the background of the development of unity, the material, social and spiritual life of man acquires significance which reveals the harmonious relation in the inner and outer states of existence. The inner development of unity is the realisation of Reality in the different stages of individual existence and the outer manifestation of unity is the development of unity in material and social life. Unity in the later states follows the unity in the inner being of man. In this context, Professor Dutta rightly observes, "Man is a microcosm of the Universe. Man contains explicitly the first three manifestations of Reality–matter, life and mind. Man has also an inner and abiding psychic entity, called the soul, around which his body, life and mind are organised into an individual entity or ego, and which stores up the individual's experience, and persists through the changes of body, life and mind."[15]

Through a change of this 'individual entity or *ego*' of man, it relates itself with others and thus expresses unity of individual with the social life, that, in the observation of Sri Aurobindo, is the expression of Reality as the divine value of unity in individual and social states of existence. Professor Dutta evaluates thus: "For Aurobindo, the Absolute is an original, unbroken unity, not a unity constructed by reason out of multiplicity; it is an unmediated unity, which can freely manifest itself, however, in countless finite expressions of itself. Moreover, Absolute Consciousness is not Thought (as in Hegel) but an inseparable unity of Thought, Will and Bliss."[16]

In the background of this analysis, it may be noted that according to Sri Aurobindo, the Unity as Absolute Reality, manifested through the 'countless finite expressions' in this world, finally reveals it as the highest value, realised in human existence as 'an inseparable unity of Thought, Will and Bliss', and thus its existence in man finally relates him with others in society for the development of unity in all, which, in the observation of Sri Aurobindo, is the Gnostic development of man and society.

Gnostic Being, as the interrelatedness of humanity and divinity, expresses the fundamental essence of all existences, because man, nature and society finally manifest the divine integrality for the fulfillment of their final end as completeness. Thus, the development of Gnostic life means the harmonious advancement of individual and social existence in the Gnostic society, where, Sri Aurobindo observes, the collective life in society follows the principle of the Gnostic individual, because the Gnostic development of society stands on the relation of unity of individual and social life.

But the Gnostic development of the collective life does not mean the abolition of individual peculiarities and particularities of different communities; it, on the other hand, develops the spirit of interrelatedness which is not dead or static, but is the expression of the dynamic divinity as a totality in diversity, based on the principles of unity as '...the Gnostic consciousness', mutuality as '...the natural result of its direct awareness of oneness in diversity', harmony as '...the inevitable power of the working of its force.'[17]

So, it may be observed that unity or harmony in society, stands on its consciousness or awareness in Gnostic being that leads to the realisation of divinity or divine value of unity which is to be expressed in social life through the development of unity in all as the reconciliation of all diversities that manifest the divinity in different degrees for the divine living on earth. The divine living in this world thus introduces completeness in the individual and social existence of man in different stages. In 'The Life Divine', Sri Aurobindo thus observes, "To become complete in being, in consciousness of being, in force of being, in delight of being and to live in this integrated completeness is the divine living."[18] This idea of completeness in the individual leads to the completeness in society, because the gnostic or divine living refers to the consciousness of all which involves the participations of materiality or sociality and universality and transcendentality in togetherness, without losing their specialty.

Transcendentality is the fundamental basis of the development of unity in individual and social life of man. Man exists in this society in the material world, so his material or bodily existence in society cannot be denied. It is to be organised consistently through the transcendence of the mere consciousness of body or narrow bodily interest, producing contradictions or evils in society. Body, on the other hand, is taken as the instrument for the expression of higher unity as Self as the Universal Consciousness of all. In this context, man also transcends the mere attachment of mind as ego, responsible for producing disunities; mind of man, on the other hand, is accepted as an instrument for the realisation of Self as 'universal I in all.' Thus, the proper meaning of transcendence is the transcendence of limitations or contradictions for their perfect organisation as the reconciliation in simultaneously in activity in human existence as the expression of universality.

Through the process of transcendence, man, in the opinion of Sri Aurobindo, can transcend the ordinary outward consciousness and thus there is an inward turning of consciousness in man through which there is the realisation of Reality as the divine value of oneness, universally present in everything. So the transcendence from the limitedness or finiteness leads to the realisation of transcendental value or infinite oneness as divine unity in being which interrelates individuality with universality or humanity with transcendental divinity. In this way, the fundamental object of Sri Aurobindo's idea of the religion of Man as the expression of God in man as the aspects of divinisation of man and humanisation of God become complete. This, according to Sri Aurobindo, is nothing but the manifestation of Godness as the divine value of unity or oneness in the form of the value of divinised humanity in human life and society. Sri Aurobindo evaluates this outlook thus: "Our aim must be perfect as God in His being and bliss is perfect, pure as He is pure; blissful as He is blissful, and, when we are ourselves siddhas in Purana *Yoga* to bring all mankind to the same divine perfection."[19]

The realisation of 'divine perfection' in individual existence thus leads to the 'divine perfection' of mankind. In the process of inner living through the inward turning of consciousness, Sri Aurobindo observes, there is a gradual expansion of ego or selfishness to selflessness and in this way there arises the inner self or universality that is the idea of unity expressed through the outward unity with others in society. So the social living of man follows the realisation of inner unity which removes the contradictions between ego or individual interest and social interest, expressed through the living with others in the society. This selfless development of man and society, according to Sri Aurobindo is purely spiritual that follows not Gnostic development of individual and society as the extension of selflessness through the manifestation of universal self as spiritual unity in all which makes man and society free from narrow selfishness or poor material interests and develops intimate relation of unity in thought and action. So universal thought potent in man, expressed through the universality in action through love and service for others in society which fulfills the universal spirit in individual and collective living. The fulfillment of this universality passes through the individual, social and universal stages of life like the realisation of perfection in the individual and social states of existence through the development of the relation of unity with others in love and finally in universal existence through the inauguration of universal humanity. This Gnostic development of human personality in individual and social or universal forms, according to Sri Aurobindo, is not mere material or social, because this outward development is poor and temporary reflections of potential universality in the inner existence of man. So, this development of human personality is Gnostic or spiritual which is a harmonious development of material, are social and universal existence of man for the integral advancement of individual, collective and finally the total existence of man revealed through the freedom in unity. This freedom is the essential natural, eternal or spiritual development of human existence that is not concerned with mere personal salvation of individual, but is concerned with the salvation of collective life in society through the freedom in equality and in justice that finally leads to the development of freedom of the total existence as the salvation of mankind through the inauguration of divinised humanity in the form of universal love and service for all. The development of this new type of humanity in the form of social and human values, presents a new type of social philosophy for the freedom of mankind as related to the freedom in human existence. This type of human freedom emerges from the intrinsic and eternal nature of man which is internally free. The freedom of man, according to Sri Aurobindo, is a natural and harmonious advancement as the Gnostic development of human nature through the realisation of transcendental value of divinised humanity for the accomplishment of universal freedom in unity of humanity and divinity in the universal existence of man that finally makes him Universal or *Superman as Superhuman* whose free existence is eternally related with the freedom of mankind. So the Gnostic development of man is the development of his individual, social and universal existences, developing freedom in his individual and social life.

In the light of this analysis, it may be noted that the Gnostic development of human freedom is the accomplishment of divine unity in his supernature which is the transcendence of ordinary values of our daily life coming from ignorance or material ego. But it may be said in this connection that this type of Gnostic development of the supernature of man is not unnatural or supernatural in Nietschean form, but it is the natural or harmonious growth of human existence, transcending ordinary material or empirical values for poor self-interest, responsible for producing contradictions or evils in society and thus through the transcendence of material or empirical nature, Sri Aurobindo observes, there is the gradual unfolding of supernature as the realisation of unified knowledge of Divine Reality that is the eternal expression of human freedom in unity of individual and collective life, manifesting a synthesis of humanity and divinity as divinised humanity.

Thus, the Gnostic development of human freedom may be termed as the divine life on earth which can be possible through the emergence of the supernature as the natural and harmonious growth of internally, mentally or spiritually productive existence of Man as *Superman or Superhuman*. The development of this productive existence means the manifestation of universality or infiniteness in him, which, on the one hand, makes man free from all types of contradictions or evils due to narrow individual interests and it, on the other hand, can also help a man to be free from all types of social, mental and spiritual alienation through the development of self-creating and self-unfolding unity of individual and social or universal states of life, revealing neither the pure or abstract unity, nor mere pluralities or diversities, but as a concrete unity–in–diversity, exhibiting the proper significance of divinity in life and existence on earth.

Thus, in and through the Gnostic development of life in the self-creative being of man as *Superman or Superhuman*, he may live in the sorrows and sufferings of society due to contradictions or evils, but he can transcend these evils through the development of creative personality, revealing perfect joy of self-creation as Infinite Bliss through which he enjoys freedom or *mukti* in this world.

It should be noted in this context, the realisation of freedom in individual existence, according to Sri Aurobindo, is not freedom of his own self, but in his freedom he is essentially related with the creative service in love for others, that, on the one hand, reveals his potent universality or infiniteness, expressing unity, and it, on the other hand, through the integral process of divine union or *Yoga* as the self-creating principle of unity, establishes freedom in unity in all as the divine life on earth*.

So Sri Aurobindo's outlook, in this context, differs from the traditional Indian system of thought as he does not accept the idea of salvation as the freedom from this worldly existence, which, according to the traditional thinkers, is unreal; creating bondage or evil. But Sri Aurobindo thinks that salvation is a state of freedom in unity as the expression of divinity in this world and worldly existence of man. This idea of salvation of Sri Aurobindo is evaluated by Dr Srivastava thus: "Salvation is not a state of freedom or escape from the bondage of nature. In the traditional systems, the soul has been conceived as a bird in the cage and salvation is freedom, escape or liberation from that cage of *Prakriti*. For Sri Aurobindo, nature is not a cage. The Nature is God, and, therefore, salvation does not consist in the escape of soul from *Prakriti* to some unknown region nor does it mean destruction of the body, life and mind of our individual. Salvation is a state in which the mind, life, body and soul get divinely transformed. It is the perfected state in which the body becomes luminous, the mind omniscient, the life immortal and the soul in union with the Supermind. Sri Aurobindo speaks of the integral salvation of an individual. To be a *Superman* is to be a god on earth. It is to be like a god and to possess the divine consciousness, power, truth, blessedness, etc. Therefore, salvation means taking a divine birth in the cosmos."[20]

Thus, in this process of developing the state of integral salvation as 'a divine birth in the cosmos', there will be the possibility of the

---

* CF. "Our union with a Being whose activity is worldwide and who dwells in the heart of humanity cannot be passive one. In order to be united with Him we have to divest our work of selfishness and become Visvakarma, -'The world worker', we must work for all. When I use the words 'for all', I do not mean for a countless number of individuals. All work that is good, however small in extent, is universal in character. Such work makes for a realisation of Visvakarma-'the world worker' who works for all. In order to be one with this Mahatma, 'The Great Soul', one must cultivate the greatness of soul which identifies itself with the soul of all people and not merely with that one's own. This helps us to understand what Buddha has described as Brahmavihara, -'living in the infinite'". Rabindranath Tagore, The Religion of Man.

life of the *Supermanhood*, when, through the supramental evolution, there will be the emergence of 'a race of supramental beings on earth' and thus finally there will be the establishment of a creative and spiritually illumined state of divine or heavenly life on earth. For this Sri Aurobindo, in his 'Savitri' states thus: "The Spirit shall take up the human play, this earthly life become the life divine."[21]

In the background of this divine life on earth, Sri Aurobindo thus emphasises the importance of individual as the integrated spiritual personality, but denies extreme *individualism*, which takes individual as ultimate being and more superior to society that is an artificial organisation of individuals. Again other political thinkers, like democrats and anarchists also put a stress on the priority of the individual freedom.

In this connection it may be pointed out further that though Sri Aurobindo emphasises the completeness of the human life, standing on a synthesis of individual and social states of existence, developing unity in society; still he rejects the extreme collectivism as it takes the importance of society as primary reality and individuals are its parts. *Marxism* and *Fascism* also advocate the superiority of state over individuals. But in order to explain the nature of the intimate and essential relation of individual and society, these extreme views about the supremacy of individual over society or state, or the supremacy of state or society over individual, are introduced. There are also many other political views like aristocracy, monarchy, oligarchy etc. But as all these views emphasise the materialistic development of man and society, the relation of individual and society, according to these views, is material or artificial and so the strict laws, regimentation etc. are to be enacted for the maintenance of order in society.

But in the opinion of Sri Aurobindo, the intimate relation of man and society, is not material or artificial, but is eternal, as it expresses Reality, both in man and society as the manifestation of social, universal and human value of divine unity. Man exists in society and he requires it for his self-development and the society or State, being an instrument, is also required for the integrated development of human personality and thus both man and society are to be harmoniously developed in different stages through the accomplishment of Reality as divine unity. So both man and society are eternally related as these are to be naturally and harmoniously developed for the integral advancement of individual and social states of existence, through the realisation of transcendental value of divinised humanity in different degrees. This eternal, human and divine relation of unity between man and society as explained by Sri Aurobindo, is evaluated by Professor Dutta thus: "Regimentation and external pressure can at best produce a uniformity, but not unity. Real unity is harmony in the free play of the many. Such a unity or harmony is the basic and spontaneous law of the spirit."[22]

This idea of 'the law of the spirit', is the central doctrine of Sri Aurobindo's philosophy, that interrelates Eastern and Western, old and modern views, in the background of a new, integrated and democratic outlook for the evaluation of the human freedom in the context of human relation. Man is not subordinate to society and society is also not under man, but both are eternally related for the perfect expression of divinity in the form of humanity which does not deny different social relations among men but organises these relations in a integral manner, revealing 'the law of the spirit' as unity. Man, in the undeveloped state of life, under different obligations and limitations, follow the rules of society, but through a gradual development of integral spirit in him in different stages, he gradually organises his physical, vital and mental being, transcending different limitations and thus he gradually becomes free through the realisation of highest human value of divinity in different degrees, that finally leads to the development of perfection in individual and social existence, revealing the universal spirit of unity in all, expressed through the human relation among men.

So the relation of man with others in society, is purely human as it can make men more intimate, and it is also divine because the individual and collective life of man realises this transcendental value of divinised humanity in different degrees till the final realisation of perfection as the unity of individuality and universality or humanity and divinity, is reached in the final state of human freedom. In 'The Human Cycle' and in 'The Ideal of Human Unity', Sri Aurobindo explains the significance of the final state of freedom in unity as the fundamental basis of the human civilisation. But modern civilisation emphasises the materialistic explanation of life and society, standing on the mechanisation or the rationalisation of values that treat man as the means, leading to disunity, or disharmony, caused by several differences or limitations of different nations, states, federations and other political organisations. But, Sri Aurobindo observes that man is the end and his relation with others in society is eternal and human, revealing the highest value of the integrated humanity as divine unity that is to be harmoniously realised by the mankind as the final end of life and existence. In the background of this observation, Sri Aurobindo explains 'The Future Society' of man thus: "The object of all society should be, therefore, and must become, as man grows conscious of his real being, nature and destiny and not as now only of a part of it, first to provide the conditions of life and growth by which individual Man, -not isolated men or a class or a privileged race, but all individual men according to their capacity, -and the race through the growth of its individuals may travel towards this divine perfection."[23]

In the context of the manifestation 'of this divine perfection' in human life and society as the harmonious development of the unity of divinity and humanity, Sri Aurobindo observes that man's relation with others in society, is not mechanical or artificial, but is natural or essential, as it stands on divine union or *Integral Yoga* that makes the religion of Man as the natural and harmonious expression of divinised humanity, complete. This outlook of Sri Aurobindo is not mere sentimental and intellectual, but it's purely human as it emphasises the essential and harmonious development of the individual and the collective life in society through an integrated way for the realisation of the value of divinised humanity in different forms of social values like equality, liberty and fraternity, expressing the divine life on earth, leading to the final freedom in unity of divinity and humanity. Sri Aurobindo evaluates thus: "It must be, secondly, as mankind generally more and more grows near to some figure of the Divine in life and more and more men arrive at it, -for the cycles are many and each cycle has its own figure of the Divine in man, -to express in the general life of mankind, the light, the power, the beauty, the harmony, the joy of the Self that has been attained and that pours itself out in a freer and nobler humanity."[24]

References

1. The Life Divine, Vol. II, pp. 888-894.
2. Nathaniel Pearson, Sri Aurobindo and the Soul Quest of Man, p. 25.
3. S. K. Maitra, An Introduction to the Philosophy of Sri Aurobindo, p. 17.
4. *Ibid*, p. 17.
5. P. Nagaraja Rao, Contemporary Indian Philosophy, p. 97.
6. Sri Aurobindo, Synthesis of *Yoga*, p. 4.
7. Keshavmurti, Sri Aurobindo–The Hope of Man, p. 451.
8. Sri Aurobindo, The Synthesis of *Yoga*, p. 49.
9. Sri Aurobindo, The Future Evolution of Man, pp. 109-113.
10. Sri Aurobindo, The Life Divine, Vol. II, p. 840.
11. Sri Aurobindo, The Synthesis of *Yoga*, p. 542.
12. Sri Aurobindo, The Future Evolution of Man, p. 120.
13. *Ibid*, p. 126.
14. *Ibid*, p. 140.
15. D.M. Dutta, The Chief Currents of Contemporary Philosophy, pp.165-166.
16. *Ibid*, p. 167.
17. The Life Divine, Vol. II, p. 901.
18. *Ibid*, p. 1025.
19. The Advent, Vol. XI, No. 2, p. 16.
20. Dr R. S. Srivastava, Contemporary Indian Philosophy, pp. 137-138.
21. Savitri, Book XI, Canto I.
22. D. M. Dutta, The Chief Currents of Contemporary Philosophy, p. 170.
23. Sri Aurobindo and Mother on the Future Society, p. 2.
24. *Ibid*, pp. 2-3.

Chapter - 3

Sri Aurobindo's Religion of Man, The *Superhuman*: A Critical and Comparative Evaluation

Part - I

Examination of the Ideas and Ways of Developing Man, The Superhuman

Sri Aurobindo, a great contemporary Indian thinker, occupies a unique position in contemporary philosophy, for initiating a comprehensive outlook of philosophy and religion through a simultaneous and progressive development of both to a new order of the philosophy of religion as the religion of Man. In the evaluation of novel thought, the idea of man has to be related to the evolutionary progress of Sri Aurobindo's different stages of life towards the process of an integral outlook, in the background of the advanced aspects and ideals of Eastern and Western thought and culture.

Thus, the development of integral view of Sri Aurobindo, in the advanced aspects of India's *Yoga* and *Tantra* and the progressive scientific perspectives of Western culture, it is found that man acquires a central position in his deliberative process as giving proper and adequate importance where his existence is taken as the synthesis of material and spiritual processes as dual expressions of the supramental process in its confronted orders, manifesting the intrinsic Nature of Man in cosmic-social process, a comprehensive religious or divine or universal nature of human existence as the proper consciousness. In this analysis of life and existence of man, Sri Aurobindo states that it is "...the attempts to know and live in the highest self, the divine, the embracing unity and to raise life in all parts to the divinest possible values."[1]

Thus, the idea of the religion of Man as taken as the universal or divine nature of man and as the art of divine living in this material world through the realisation of divine value of unity, potent in him, Sri Aurobindo opposes the traditional or ordinary view of religion, where religion is taken as the imposition of value on human life. But he observes that religion is not imposition, but it is the natural expression of human existence, manifesting the human values. Thus, putting an emphasis on the explanation of the meaning of religion as the natural expression of the nature and existence of man, Sri Aurobindo introduces human outlook in an integral development of his new order of the integral thought about man as the religion of *Superman as Superhuman*.

In the background of his integral view, Sri Aurobindo places religion as an evolutionary progress where religion does not stand as hindrance but as closely related process to the advancement of life to an integral prospect.

But religion, in the earlier cultural context, with its ideological frame of reference in the western–sense, entertained same abstract ideas, which resulted in conflicting attitude, throughout its medieval period. This conflicting attitude ingrained in religious consciousness, created the conflicts among the various religions then prevalent, extending the progressive aspects of scientific and philosophical ideas of man.

In order to be free from this ideological conflict of the Western early religious consciousness–Sri Aurobindo tries to liberate religion as understood in The West in general by drawing attention to the transcendental order of deliberations developed in India throughout the centuries where there is also a stress on a disciplined way of life, not alone of mere consciousness. Indian Philosophy and Religion, where also religion is not placed beside or beyond the human existence, but placed in the concrete realities of day-to-day life. In the opinion of Sri Aurobindo, religious experience is the inner energy of man that stimulates the material and mental states of man in simultaneity. The spiritual energy in man stimulates his material and mental states in togetherness, revealing 'The Human Aspiration' for the harmonious development of his creative personality in many-dimensional experiential process of Man as philosopher, scientist, social reformer or as humanist, through the progressive consciousness of some human values in individual and social life.

In the analysis of the nature of human value, Sri Aurobindo does not describe it as not merely material or social, but as also spiritual or divine that harmonises different values of life for the development of each in its manifestation of a progressive integral consciousness beyond each. In and through this manifestation of inner integral spirituality in man, he becomes free from the specific restrictions of material or empirical ego. This spirituality, according to Sri Aurobindo, is not to be confused with mere *idealism, intellectualism, religionism or ethicalism*, because, it is not a mere creed or belief, to be imposed on man, but it is a natural or harmonious expression as total transformation of the whole being by the divinity or universal Self which is already involved in Man leading to the sustaining and developing an individual and society in togetherness. Different religions, mystic views, spiritual thoughts etc. may help or inspire a man to work for the manifestation of this comprehensive order of spirituality, potential in him.

In the context of this analysis we may meet the charge against spirituality if held as a fixed concept. From this perspective the critics point out that too much emphasis on spirituality creates confusions regarding the problems of life and existence instead of solving the problems of life.

This criticism against spirituality from an ideological frame of mind, according to Sri Aurobindo, is due to the misapprehension of its nature, as a dynamic consciousness, sustaining and directing entire life and existence. In '*The Life Divine*', he observes that spirituality as dynamic and directive process is, '...to create a new foundation of our being and our life and knowledge'. For the interpretation of the character of this new foundation he refers to the life of a mystic, who tries to detach himself from the limitation or narrow way of living, by a development of universal spirit of love. So the spiritual man is not concerned with the selfishness, he tries to overcome it through the expression of his inner spiritual nature, intimately related with all. A spiritually cognizant person stands on the inner realisation of the universal spirit in man, manifesting the spirituality as eternal unity which vibrates the inner and external processes of life and existence.

So, in the background of this analysis of the spirituality as the harmonious development of internal and external or social states of existence, we can also meet another charge against this outlook. Against this view some critics may observe that as it is an inner realisation of inner spirit which is found in the inner realisations of mystics, it may be said that this type of inner realisation makes truth purely subjective, and that, at the same time, become different and variable due to subjective variations, caused by the different types of realisations by different mystics or persons. But Sri Aurobindo does not stand for the individual mental order of a personality but a supramental process beyond restricted mentality.

Thus, in the context of this analysis of spirituality, representing truth as an integral consciousness in diversity, Sri Aurobindo determines its significance in life, referring to it as the standard of life where the spiritual nature of Truth or Reality is taken as value which has both empirical and transcendental references. Truth or Reality as transcendental value is to be realised through the different states of individual and social existence as different empirical values as the different stages of manifestations of the transcendental value as unity. Thus, in the context of this transcendental unity, the realisation of this highest value is possible in the human life in this empirical world, manifested as empirical values or human values, towards the realisation of final state of completeness or harmony in individual and social life.

In the light of this analysis of the spiritual nature of the human existence as the expression of transcendental value of unity through the appearances of different human values in different states of the empirical existence of man, Sri Aurobindo also evaluates the eternal or essential meaning of the expression of human nature as the religion of Man which is the faith on values and expression of values in different stages, in the analysis of this spiritual and humanitarian view of Sri Aurobindo's idea of the religion as the religion of Man and in this state he accepts the traditional meaning of religion as the faith in values. But if the meaning of religion is taken in this sense, it may be argued against this idea that it confuses religion with fanaticism as the seat of these values. Professor Maitra points out, "Religion and fanaticism are alike, so far as faith is concerned, but differs in the objects towards which their respective faiths are directed, for while the one faith is directed towards values, the other faith is directed towards anti-values."[2] But this view as entertained here is ideo-centric and not a supra-conscious process as Sri Aurobindo develops throughout.

To dispel this confusion, and to make religion free from fanaticism in general, Sri Aurobindo introduces his integral view and method in the analysis of the religion as the religion of Man. In his integral approach to this meaning of religion, it is not a mere or a specific blind faith on value, but this faith stands for an integral super-consciousness which is involved in all orders of confronted existential process from Spirituality to Materiality with a continuity. Again mere exclusive reason or rational query, cannot explain the nature and existence of value as a whole, because its approach is also limited, not integral nor comprehensive. Like Hegel and Hegelians, Sri Aurobindo, though accepts the rational value of religion and its rational basis on the history of human life, still his emphasis is always on a 'supra-rational', 'supra-conscient' or more comprehensive and integral outlook of religion for the explanation of the greater and wider purpose of human life in nature. This super-conscious approach was completely absent in the ideo-centric thinkers to the stage of Hegel or his followers in Western thought.

For the interpretation of this outlook of religion, Sri Aurobindo emphasises the religion as the religion of Man which is a directive consciousness and not as a static notion or a faith, which, according to him, spirituality is sustaining process stretching from the spirit to nature to the stage of Materiality. For the evaluation of the nature in this integral frame, Sri Aurobindo emphasises the meaning of religion as the existence of transcendental value of interrelatedness which is to be expressed in life and existence as different human values in different stages, for the upliftment of all basic processes–to a possibility beyond their restrictness.

This meaning of Sri Aurobindo's religion of Man as a directive possibility of values with existence is also related to the value with expression that is natural and harmonious. In the background of this analysis, he avoids the artificial approach to religion as an ideological imposition of something on man through different artificial procedure like different ritualistic performances, ceremonies, etc. but Sri Aurobindo observes that religion is not the imposition of values, but it is integral to all orders of experiential–and its concern is a natural harmonious development or expression of values in human life as a whole.

So, the idea of value in this sense, is essentially related with the human nature and existence, where it is not imposed from outside, but on the other hand, it is the ever present vibrant principle of human nature, leading to progressive integrality.

In order to explain the nature or existence of value as an integral process as the highest state of Reality, expressed through the divinity in man, Sri Aurobindo does not take it as imposition of something on man, but it, on the other hand, is the realisation of human nature as in its entirety.

Thus, in the background of this analysis of Sri Aurobindo, the proper meaning of religion is the realisation of the divinity in life and existence and so, religion, according to him, is inextricably related to a directive process towards a Supreme Consciousness or Reality. This spiritual realisation as the expression of inner divinity harmoniously develops the material, mental and spiritual existence of man to a common prospect beyond their restrictness. This is the realisation of the highest state of unity as highest value or reality in the deeper or inner spirit of man.

In the context of this meaning of the religion of Man as the inner realisation of the value of unity as Reality, Sri Aurobindo denounces the artificial meaning and methods of religion as the worshipping of God or Reality by man, as devotee. Thus, Sri Aurobindo's idea of the religion of Man opposes the traditional views or common features of different religions like different methods of worshipping personal and impersonal God. Different religions of the world thus introduces different artificial religious rights and ceremonies for worshipping God or gods as they are all ideo-centric and restrictive. But Sri Aurobindo does not prescribe any such rights and ceremonies or artificial methods for worshipping God or Ultimate Reality. Different methods of worship create differences and increase discrepancies, instead of developing unity, which is to be realised in the inner universal nature of man. This human nature is eternally and essentially related to religious experience as a whole. In the context of the realisation and expression of this highest state of unity or universality as the divine value of unity in inner and intrinsic nature of man, Sri Aurobindo points out, "It is not sufficient to worship Krishna, Christ or Buddha without, if there is not the revealing and the formulation of the Buddha, the Christ or Krishna in ourselves."[3] In other words, it is one of the comprehensive process realisable by each person and the world as a whole as a presence.

Thus, in the background of this idea of divine value in this comprehensive psychic-cosmic sense–and in the context of Sri Aurobindo's idea of the religion of Man as the realisation of unity in human existence is the harmonious expression of human nature. Here, he like Bradley, accepts the differences and also emphasises the *Yoga* or Union as a psychical process of going beyond the diversities or differences in life and society. In the context of Sri Aurobindo's idea of realisation as the culmination in *Yoga* or divine union, we can meet the change against his idea of religion. This may be criticised in the traditional sense of religion, for it does not prescribe any method of worshipping God through which there will be the fulfillment of religious aspirations. But Sri Aurobindo points out that the fundamental object of religion is not to create differences in life, due to artificial approaches or methods of worshipping God through different rites or ceremonies in different religions, but religion or religious aspirations, according to him, is the human aspiration, which, on the other hand, is the realisation of divinity in man which is not the introduction of divinity on man but is the expression of godness in man through the manifestation of divine or spiritual unity in life. This, according to Sri Aurobindo, is 'Man's highest aspiration', which is to "...indicate the gradual unveiling of the Spirit within, the preparation of a higher life upon earth."[4] The realisation of unity, thus in different stages of life as the expression of Reality in different degrees as 'The preparation of a higher life', according to Sri Aurobindo, this is the transformation, psychisation, integration and perfect or complete union. This, according to Sri Aurobindo, is not imposition, but is a natural or harmonious expression or the development of human nature in an essential process of *Yoga* or union that leads to the completion of life and society through the reconciliation of contradictions or differences in unity or harmony. Introduction of this unity in man and world, according to Sri Aurobindo, is not mere material or mental progress, but it is a spiritual or harmonious development of life and existence through the realisation of the total nature of Reality.

So the religion, according to Sri Aurobindo, is the realisation of universality expressed through socio-moral, socio-cultural or religious or philosophical values in life, finally culminating in *Yoga* or unity with the divine process. This is an integral approach of Sri Aurobindo to the idea of religion as the expression of unity or universality in and through the process of *Yoga* or divine union as the realisation of Reality in different orders from matter to mind and beyond them all to a supramental and mental processes.

In the background of this integral outlook of Sri Aurobindo's idea of the religion of Man, we can also meet the charge against his idea that he confuses the idea of religion with philosophy and ethics or morality. But in the context of Sri Aurobindo's integral analysis of religion, ethics and philosophy, as it is observed that these are nothing but the expression of different values, revealing the nature of Reality in life in different degrees, the confusions and conflicts among these systems are apparent. The conflict among these systems are due to an emphasis on religion as a seed of spiritual values, philosophy as a seed of rational values and ethics as a seed of socio-moral values. But Sri Aurobindo's integral approach to Reality referred to an inter-relatedness of all these values, manifesting the total nature of Reality in human life that leads to a synthesis of thought, emotion and work which can be expressed as the philosophy as the thought or knowledge of Reality. Religion as the realisation of Reality and ethics as expression of Reality in different socio-moral activities through selfless service for mankind in love. So it may be noted in this connection that in this integral explanation of Sri Aurobindo, philosophy, religion and morality are finally transformed into an integrated in spiritual experience of man as the integration of matter, mind and spirit for the harmonious development of human existence as Universal Man. In the process of divine union or *Yoga* as the knowledge, faith and living realisation of values in unity.

In the context of this harmonious development of human nature towards the highest state of the realisation of unity and universality as integral consciousness and inter-relatedness, the idea of science as a modern approach to life and existence, is becoming free from contradictions which are created by its emphasis on the mere material explanation of man in the world. But the material explanations of science, in modern times, are acquiring more significance through the development of universal outlook of man that helps it to explain the significance of nature and existence of human beings in this world in the background of integrality. Science has now acquired a new meaning- "the time has come to realise that an interpretation of the universe–even a positivist one–remains unsatisfying unless it covers the interior as well as the exterior of things; mind as well as matter. The true physics is that which will, one day, achieves the inclusion of man in his wholeness in a coherent picture of the universe"[5]. In the background of this interrelatedness of processes from Nature to Man, this scientific approach to the totality of man as coherently related with the world, the significance of Sri Aurobindo's integral approach to man and Reality can be evaluated. This finally examines the scientific outlook of man as the natural and harmonious expression of Reality as universal unity which finally identifies the explanation of science with that of religion or spirituality, because the fundamental objects of these ideas are to explain the integral existence of universal nature of man for this Bacon emphasises 'a little science makes man atheist, whereas a great deal of science turns the man's thought to religion'. So the advancement of science or scientific outlook of man leads to realisation of the intrinsic nature of human existence as the expression of the proper religion of Man, which, in the observation of Sri Aurobindo, is the spiritual development of universal unity of materiality and transcendentality.

In order to explain the nature of this realisation, Sri Aurobindo evaluates it neither as mere material, nor as mere mental, but it is spiritual which is the harmonious development of both material and mental states towards the realisation of the transcendental value of unity through the transcendence of different limitations and contradictions of material and mental states in and through their reconciliation in unity. Sri Aurobindo thus observes that man has to transcend the physical or material, vital and mental states and through the transcendence of their limitations there will be an inauguration of the universal spirit to control the lower nature. In this way, through a process of transcendence both individual and Universal Consciousness will acquire the completeness in a deeper synthesis as the evaluation of Universal Man as *Superman or Superhuman.* So, Man's evolution, according to Sri Aurobindo, is not an evolution in ignorance or through inconscience but it is an evolution of the knowledge of Reality towards the realisation of completeness of superconscience. It may be noted that there will be a direct confrontation with a transcendent yet an all pervasive principle–which is supramaterial and supramental process of developing all to a possibility beyond the existent order by way of total transformation.

In the context of this analysis of the transformation of inconscience or ignorance to knowledge of superconscience, Sri Aurobindo also meets the charges of skeptics who observes that material existence, being essentially blind, dark and inconscience and mental existence also in embodied or material stage, being in ignorance, there is no possibility of the transformation of these states to superconscience. In his reply to this criticism, Sri Aurobindo firmly states that ignorance cannot be '…the whole meaning, substance and power of the world-manifestation', it, on the other hand, is a mere part of the World–Nature. In the lower stage of existence in the material world, it may exist in a part, but matter also, in the observation of Sri Aurobindo, is the veiled conscience, which appears in this stage of self–limiting consciousness that cannot express its nature fully. But this potential consciousness in material and also in mental states gradually reveal its nature through the transcendence of limitation or contradiction due to ignorance or inconscience, and thus through this process of transcendence and through the realisation of the knowledge of Reality, there is a total transformation of the existence of man, which, in the observation of Sri Aurobindo, as the evolution of *Superman or Superhuman* through the evolution of material, vital, mental, supramental stages of life and existence. Like modern scientists–Sri Aurobindo visualises a comprehensive spiritual order from matter to man as mental.

But in the examination of this evolution of *Superman or Superhuman* in the human existence beyond the different dimensions of mental orders–in this material world as the evolution superconscience–in the scheme of Nature, a charge of determinism is raised against this idea because this idea of evolution of life is not a reductive process, it is a move towards a totally transcendent order, beyond the reach of any specific material or mental order. Sri Aurobindo meets the charge through an explanation of the inner meaning of the evolution of human nature as the change of the limitation of different states through the realisation of the proper knowledge of Reality as the divine value of unity, which, he observes, manifests the fundamental object and the true significance of evolution as the creative integrality. This, according to Sri Aurobindo, is the natural development of man as the realisation of divinity in him, which may be called as a practical approach to Reality and is not a theoretical one which is to be imposed on man from outside and man's nature is not also to be determined by this process of artificial imposition.

So this process of developing the transcendent divine order of man as the directive activity of *Superman or Superhuman* in the dual orders of involution and evolution is not artificial, it is natural, essential spontaneous and harmonious, not in any specific but in a comprehensive sense. This type of teleological evolution of life and existence, may be contradicted by the materialists who observe that evolutionary process in human existence is purely material as an activity of blind and unconscious energy, working mechanically. In support of this material or mechanical approach, Herbert Spencer also accepts the mechanical theory of evolution. Darwin, a renowned biologist, also thinks that the evolution of human life is to be explained with reference to a series of accidental variations and natural selections which are purely unconscious and mechanical. This process, according to Lamarck, is a hereditary adjustment of human being with the environment, which, in the observation of Lamarckians, is blind and unconscious response of man to the environment under the mechanical laws of environment. Karl Marx also accepts the materialistic account of life and also denies the teleological evolution of man.

In reply to this oppositions, Sri Aurobindo points out the evolution of man is not to be perfectly explained in the background of blind matter only, because matter cannot explain the significance of the material existence of man which is for the fulfillment of higher purpose of life. Matter itself cannot explain the purpose of the material existence of man, because matter cannot be explained by itself as it is not self-explained. In '*The Life Divine*', Sri Aurobindo explains thus: 'Matter itself can no longer be explained by matter alone, for it does not appear to be self-explained'.

Again if we try to explain the nature of human existence in the context of this blind and unconscious matter, and if human life is taken as the series of mechanical variations, then we cannot explain the deeper significance of the evolution of man as the emergence of the superior type of being, expressing human unity in different states of life that reveals the teleological progress of human existence for the harmonious development of material or individual and social or universal existence of man.

In the context of this harmonious and integral development of the individual and social life, man is distinct from mere external process of expressing mechanical relation, revealed through the human organism as the mechanical aggregates. Man is also distinct from an isolated individual, as nothing but the aggregate of mental properties. But human organism, according to Sri Aurobindo, is neither a mere material aggregate, nor mere a mental aggregate, it, on the other hand, is a creative synthesis which is unique in character. So the creativity in man is the uniqueness of his being which is something more than mere material and mental aggregates, and it, on the other hand, is not the rejection of the two but is a harmonious development of these two states.

In the evaluation of this creative outlook of man, we may refer to the idea of Bergson, a great French Philosopher, who mentions that evolution is neither mechanical nor teleological, but creative. It is neither the mechanical selection and elimination of fit and unfit individuals with favourable or unfavourable variations which Darwin called natural selection, nor it is a teleological advancement towards any fixed goal, but it, in the opinion of Bergson, is a vital urge or *Elan Vital*, which perennially grows and freely evolves in a new creative process. In the line of these creative outlook, Lloyd Morgan and Alexander developed the doctrine of emergent evolution, which is similar to the creative evolution of Bergson as both this views observed that new forms of existence are evolved from the old materials. But the development of this new form of existence, according to Bergson's doctrine of creative evolution, is an absolutely new creation of the vital urge, which, according to critics, can neither be conceived nor be rationally explained if the evolution of the life and existence are taken as a continuous flow of entirely new and free creations. For this, Morgan and Alexander's doctrine of emergent evolution points out that the emergence of the new form of existence is due to a more complex organisation of the old materials that requires the interrelation of many constituents in a novel form which is not repetitive in character. Evolution thus is the emergence of a series of related new forms or new organisations as new states of existence from which again a new form of something emerges. In this process of emergence, it is thus observed that life emerges from matter, and mind emerges from light as the new stages of existence. Regarding the creative urge as the cause of the emergents, Morgan observes the existence of power is at the root of evolution, which, according to him, is Activity, Mind or God. He writes, 'I acknowledge, God is the Nisus through whose Activity emergents emerge, and the whole course of emergent evolution is directed'. So Morgan posits *Nisus* or God and Bergson places *Elan Vital* at the beginning of the evolution of the creative states of human life, but Alexander points out that *Space–Time* is the fundamental base from which matter, life, mind emerge for the emergence of the higher category of Deity. So, according to Alexander, the emergence of Deity is the final end of emergent evolution: "The world in its infinity tends towards infinite Deity, or is pregnant with it, but infinite Deity does not exist."[6]

In the analysis of Sri Aurobindo's idea of the evolution of the creative spirit and the creative existence of man, we get the synthesis of the ideas of creative and emergent evolution. The significance of the idea of the emergent evolution, stands on the process of forward–looking which lies in the recognition of the novelty and uniqueness of life and mind. But the idea of the forward-looking as a process of developing future end or good, without teleology, makes both these doctrines of emergent and creative evolution inexplicable and fictitious. For this, Sri Aurobindo's idea of evolution of man is a teleological progress, but it is not determined by the idea of any fixed goal of life. It, on the other hand, is a spiritual progress which is the realisation of the Universal Consciousness, potent in man and nature. Evolution means the realisation of the Universal Spirit or consciousness as the fundamental power or *Shakti* which is to be manifested in the different states of life as the teleological progress of life and existence towards the accomplishment of the final state of unity. In the background of the development of this highest state of unity, evolution is not either to start with the universal idea as *Nisus* of Morgan or *Elan Vital* of Bergson, or to end with *Deity* of Alexander, but according to Sri Aurobindo, it is extended with Universal Consciousness manifested in different states in different degrees.

In the evolution of man, there is a gradual realisation of perfection, potential in him, towards the final state of unity that requires the integral development of material, vital, mental and supramental states of human existence as the synthesis of individuality, sociality and universality, as the expression of spirituality or divinity in man. In the background of this existence of creative consciousness of unity in man as the expression of divinity, the evolution of man is taken by Sri Aurobindo as something more than mere blind mechanical or teleological progress of existence.

Man, according to Sri Aurobindo, is not the mechanical aggregate of external relations or parts like a machine, or is not determined by any fixed ideal or blind teleology, man, on the other hand, is a deeper synthesis of both external and internal states of existence that leads to the creative development and creative synthesis of different states for the completeness in unity as eternally extended with universality.

In the context of the analysis of this idea of human organism as creative synthesis as more than mechanical relation, we may refer to the idea of Haldane who points out, "....that the organism is something more than a machine, in the sense that it has unity of type which the machine lacks."[7] In the background of this evaluation of human existence, the idea of Karl Marx may also be directly referred to. Marx also opposes the mechanical approach to human existence and thus observes the existence of something in man that prepares him to select something and to reject others for the adjustment with the environment. The progress of this something in man, according to Marx, is dialectical which is not to be confused with mechanical approach to the human life, but this, something in man, in his opinion, is not also spiritual, as Sri Aurobindo observes. Thus, Marx's idea of man differs from that of Sri Aurobindo, because Marx accepts material account of human life and he thinks that man is a socio-economic and socio-political being, guided by the economic and political laws directly and by the laws of nature indirectly through which man freely constructs and reforms the history of his existence in society in different degrees. This type of free existence of man in society under socio-economic and socio-political laws, according to Sri Aurobindo, is also determined or mechanical which makes man limited and finite. So the free existence of man in society, is for the realisation of the higher freedom, that, on one hand, expresses the different states of the free existence of man in different degrees, and it, on the other hand, means the realisation of infinite or universal nature of human existence in different stages towards the realisation of the final state of human freedom in unity. So in this context both Marx and Sri Aurobindo refer to the different stages of human freedom which makes the socio-historical existence of man, more significant. Dr Chattopadhyay thus points out, "Both Sri Aurobindo and Karl Marx agree, of course in different ways, that man is the author of his socio-historical destiny, but not solely."[8]

But in the context of unity as the highest state of human freedom, Sri Aurobindo points out that the mere material or empirical account of man refers to the one-sided and incomplete approach to existence, and thus Sri Aurobindo's idea of the evolution of man is the expression of spiritual teleology which expresses the deeper relatedness in human existence in integral manner; that, in one hand, asserts the human existence under natural and social laws, and then, on the other hand, makes him conscious of his being as eternally guided by the laws of nature and society which again are nothing but the expression of the Universal Consciousness. The realisation of this Universal Consciousness, finally makes man intimate with nature and society, which expresses the significance of human freedom as freedom in unity in all. Thus, the deeper significance of the history of human existence in this context of human freedom in unity, according to Sri Aurobindo, is expressed, not merely through the material existence, manifested in external reactions only, but through the discovery of inner laws, manifesting the inner relation of unity in different stages that finally synthesises the material and individual, social and universal states of human existence towards the development of the highest state of human freedom in unity.

This integral approach of Sri Aurobindo to the deeper existence of man as the synthesis of external and internal states as the unity of materiality and spirituality which finally leads to the realisation of the potential universality in man as his self-realisation and self-consciousness of his total being as the unity of material, vital, mental and supramental states of existence. For the gradual development of these states of life, Sri Aurobindo emphasises the process of self-transcendence as the transcendence of the limitations or contradictions of particular limited state of existence in the background of the realisation of the transcendental value of unity as Reality. This, according to Sri Aurobindo, is an eternal and spiritual process of union as *Yoga* which is fundamentally concerned not merely with the faith of value, but with its realisation in human life as the expression of different human values through different human methods of love and service of humanity. In this integral process of *Yoga*, there will be the development of eternal or divine unity in man, expressed through the intimate relation of unity with others, developing the relation of the universal brotherhood on earth which finally leads to the inauguration of Universal Man as *Superman or Superhuman* in the individual as the divinity in human existence, leading to the development of the divine life on earth, expressing human unity. This process of developing divine unity in human existence, may be called as a creative synthesis. In the analysis of Sri Aurobindo's idea of the integral existence of man, we may refer to the view of William Patten, who observes that there is a universal compulsion to the constructive action in the inner state of the evolution of human existence which is a creative movement for construction and organisation of reality as self-preservation, self-sacrifice and co-operation. This creative process, present in the evolution of inorganic, organic, mental and social states, represents the methods of mutual service or co-operation.[9]

This creative being of man, as evaluated by Sri Aurobindo as the transcendence of finiteness for the realisation of infiniteness or universality, is the proper nature or religion of Man as the eternal expression of divinity; which has a similarity with the idea of other contemporary Indian thinkers, like Rabindranath and Swami Vivekananda and others. Both Rabindranath and Swami Vivekananda admit that the essential nature of religion of Man is to express divinity through the human process of love and service of humanity. This human process develops the divinity in man because God exists in man as Love or Bliss. For this Vivekananda points out that, to love man is to love God.[10] Rabindranath writes, "Whatever I can offer to God, I offer to man and to God I give whatever I can give to man. I make God man and man God."[11] As these thinkers recognise man as the expression of love and God as perfect Bliss or *Anandam*, so both can be intimate with each other in and through love. Rabindranath thinks that this ideal of love is purely human that makes man Divine or Universal and also makes God human. But Vivekananda takes love as power which is to be developed in a spiritual manner through the spiritual processes of *Yoga* as *Jnana, Karma and Bhakti.* Like Tagore, though Sri Aurobindo recognises Reality as *Anandam* still he accepts primal Reality as *Shakti* or Dynamic Divine and Cosmic Divine. Cosmic Divine works or adjusts in the present circumstances for the realisation of the Transcendent Divine: "….the cosmic wheel is working towards the eventual realisation of the will of Transcendent Divine."[12]

Thus, in the analysis of the primal nature of Reality as *Shakti* or Dynamic and Cosmic Divine in the world process for the realisation of the supreme state of Reality as Transcendent Divine, Sri Aurobindo explains fully the nature of Absolute Reality as *Saccidananda* as Existence–Consciousness–Force–Bliss. Though Absolute is fundamentally Pure Existence or Being, still motion or energy also is Reality, and so Force is taken as Reality which is Becoming. But this Force, according to Sri Aurobindo, is not unconscious and thus it is not identified with the idea of blind material force in Western Materialism, which produces consciousness; and is not also to be similar to the *Sankhya* doctrine of unconscious *Prakriti* as the basis of material force. Sri Aurobindo thus observes that Force as Reality is conscious and the conscious Force is inherent in Pure Existence or *Sat* which as the Dynamic Divine becomes the fundamental basis of the world process and appears as the Mother. The Mother as Dynamic Divine as transcendent, universal and individual forms. Sri Aurobindo writes, "transcendent, the original supreme Shakti, she stands above the worlds and links the creation to the ever unmanifest mystery of the Supreme. Universal, the cosmic *Mahashakti*, she creates all these beings and contains and enters, supports and conducts all these million processes and forces. Individual, she embodies the power of these vaster ways of her existence, makes them living and near to us and mediates between the human personality and the divine Nature."[13] The eternal purpose of this development of Reality in different forms in different degrees, is finally to manifest itself as Bliss. In the manifestation of Reality as Bliss in this world, the finite world process becomes complete and in this process the finite can transcend its finiteness through the eternal share of Bliss as perfection in life and existence.

In response to the criticism against the eternal manifestation of Reality as Bliss in this world with contradictions or evils, pains and sufferings, Sri Aurobindo points out that the existence of evil in the material world is not contrast with the Universal Bliss as Reality. But Bliss as final perfection or completeness, is the reconciliation of all contradictions or evils in the supreme Unity, in the context of which all pains and sufferings are relative or conditional. Like Mackenzie, Bosanquet and Bradley, Sri Aurobindo also observes that these contradictions as the relative states of life and world are not ultimate characters of Reality. Reality is free from contradictions which is wider and comprehensive consciousness, making us conscious about these relative states of conditions, revealing the Bliss-Self as *Anandam* in us. For the realisation of this Supreme Reality as Bliss or *Anandam* in man as the inauguration of divinity in man, is a spiritual process of developing an intermediate selective principle in man that is fundamentally necessary; and which, according to Sri Aurobindo, is not merely material, vital or mental, but is a supramental awakening of *Shakti* through a spiritual process of *Yoga*. *Yoga*, according to Sri Aurobindo, is a process of opening the doors of body, life, mind and soul for 'The supramental change' which according to Sri Aurobindo, "....is a thing decreed and inevitable in the evolution of the earth consciousness..."[14]

So in the context of this analysis of Reality as Bliss and its realisation in man on earth as the consciousness of the highest value of unity, through the supramental change in the spiritual process of *Yoga*, makes man Divine, that, according to Sri Aurobindo, is an essential process of developing the divinity of man as *Superman or Superhuman* in the individual existence. But the realisation of Reality as Bliss in man, according to Rabindranath, is possible through the human method of disinterested love and service of humanity, which is a socio-cultural procedure of developing universality in man as Universal Man. Gandhiji in his '*Young India*' also writes 'God is Truth and Love' and can be perfectly realised through love and non-violence as the socio-moral process of disinterested service of humanity.

So for the realisation of the highest value of divinity in man as the inauguration of Man in human existence, Tagore and Gandhiji prescribe the socio-cultural and socio-moral procedures of human life. This, in the analysis of Vivekananda and Sri Aurobindo, is spiritual, which, in the interpretation of Vivekananda, is supra-moral and the evaluation of Sri Aurobindo, is supra-mental development of human existence. About this process of life, Sri Aurobindo observes that it is an eternal and natural expression of being as universal religion of Man which is an inauguration of Man in the individual existence, which, in the opinion of Sri Aurobindo, is the fundamental development of the universal existence of man as *Superman or Superhuman*.

References

1. The Renaissance in India, p. 80.
2. S.K. Maitra, Studies in Sri Aurobindo's Philosophy, p. 49.
3. The Synthesis of *Yoga*, p. 74.
4. The Human Aspiration, The Future Evolution of Man, p. 23.
5. Teilhard De Chardin, The Phenomenon of Man, pp. 35-36.
6. Space, Time and Deity, Vol. II, p. 365.
7. J. B. S. Haldane, The Marxist Philosophy and the Sciences, p. 104.
8. D. P. Chattopadhyay, Sri Aurobindo on Man, p. 41.
9. The Grand Strategy of Evolution, pp. 32-34, Introduction to Philosophy, Chapter IX, XI.
10. Jive Prem Kare Yei Jan Sei Jan Seviche Isvar.
11. 'Devatare Jaha Dite Pari....Devatare Priya Kari Priyere Devata.'
12. Sri Aurobindo, The Riddle of this World (First Impression), p. 73.
13. The Mother, p. 37.
14. The Mother, pp. 83-84.

Part - II

An Integral Development of the Theory of Creative Man and the Philosophy of Humanism

In the evaluation of the nature of the universal religion, it is observed that it is the essential development of the universality in man through the realisation of human value of unity as highest Reality, expressing the divinity of man, in the human process of socio-cultural, socio-moral and spiritual process of love and service of mankind for the expression and the development of the highest value of humanity on earth. Thus, it is observed that man is taken as the fundamental medium for the realisation of value of humanity, developing unity on earth.

In the context of this analysis it may be observed that man is taken as the fundamental medium for the realisation of the value of humanity, developing human unity as the establishment of the highest ideal of *Humanism* on earth. In the evaluation of the nature of this value of humanity and the ideal of *Humanism*, we may refer to the doctrine of *homomensura*, given by Protagoras, which takes man as the measure of all things. This idea of Protagoras places individual man as the medium of measuring everything that leads to the development of individual interest as the idea of individual good which is in contrast with collective interest or social good. So the Protagorean doctrine in the first stage, though created a way towards *Humanism*, still its emphasis on individual man, finally compelled Plato and others to transcend this man-centred idea as narrow individuality. Individual man suffers from many limitations or contradictions for his individual interest, so he should be free from these contradictions under the influence of social good as the ideal of humanity which is to be interpreted by August Comte, a well-known Positivist, as 'the *religion of humanity*'. John Stuart Mill also supports this idea and in his 'Three Essays on Religion', he points out, 'The essence of religion is the strong and earnest direction of the emotions and desires towards an ideal object, recognised as of the highest excellence, and as rightfully paramount over all selfish objects of desire. This condition is fulfilled by the *Religion of Humanity* in as eminent a degree, and in as high a sense, as by the supernatural religions even in their best manifestation, and far more so than in any of their others.'

This idea of the *religion of humanity*, as founded by Comte and supported by Mill, stands on the realisation of the social value of humanity in the social life as the collective existence of man which may be explained as the socio-moral procedure of life through the service of mankind for the welfare of the people in society. Karl Marx, Engels and others though reject the importance of religion on human life, still they accept the significance of the ideal of humanity in life, expressed through the service of mankind. This socio-moral approach to the ideal of humanity related to the collective life of man in this sensual world, makes its nature more limited and finite, suffering from the contradictions and limitations of finite life of individuals in this material world. For this Max Planc criticises the positivistic approach with reference to the supersensual world, which, according to Huxley, Herbert Spencer and other Agnostics, is expressed as the ideal of divinity through matter, energy, motion and consciousness.

In the context of this analysis we may refer to the humanitarian view of Buddha, who emphasises the ideal of humanity without any reference to God or ultimate Reality, but still he explains the highest state of humanity as the expression of absolute pleasure in the state of *Nirvana*, manifesting the divinity of man in this world. This divinity of man, expressed through the humanity in love and service of mankind, manifests the infiniteness or universality in human existence, which is evaluated by Tagore thus: "...Buddha's idea of the infinite was not the idea of a spirit of an unbounded cosmic activity, but the infinite whose meaning is in the positive ideal of goodness and love, which cannot be otherwise than human."[1]

This ideal, referring to the infiniteness in man, manifested in the highest state of human existence as unity or oneness in absolute pleasure, is finally evaluated by Tagore thus: "it is not the magnitude of extension but an intense quality of harmony which evokes in us the positive sense of the infinite in our joy, in our love. For *advaitam* is *Anandam*; the infinite One is infinite Love."[2] So the cultivation of infiniteness in the finite existence through the human process of love and service, according to Tagore, is the '*meditation on humanity*', which is essential for the introduction of the idea of his religion of Man as the manifestation of "The idea of the humanity of our God, or the divinity of Man."[3]

In the development of the idea of the religion of Man as the synthesis of the ideals of humanity and divinity, Tagore thus unites the humanitarian aspects of the *religion of humanity*, presented in the thoughts of Comte, Mill, Buddha and others and superhuman and divine aspects of the religion of mysticism, presented in the thoughts of Bergson, *Bauls, Sufis* and other Indian and Western mystics. Tagore's idea of humanity, presented in his religion of Man, is the reconciliation of Infinite and finite in human existence and thus transcends the limits of material or narrow human interests, advocated by the *religion of humanity*. Again through this reconciliation of Infinite and finite in man in and through the human process of love and service of mankind, developing his idea of Socio-Cultural *Humanism*, Tagore determines the relation of unity of God and man, presenting the ideals of the 'humanity of God' and the 'divinity of man' and thus also crosses the limits of mere individual or personal realisation of divinity by a complete detachment of man from the world which is supported by the religion of mysticism. Tagore's idea of the religion of Man, on the other hand, is the divinisation of man and humanisation of God, manifested in the highest state of human freedom in unity in individual and social existence, developing infiniteness in man as Universal Man.

This process of developing divinised humanity, according to Sri Ramakrishna and Swami Vivekananda, is not completely possible through a socio-moral and socio-cultural process; it, on the other hand, is a spiritual process of developing universality in man through *Yoga* or divine union, which, according to Swami Vivekananda is a supramoral process of developing spiritual brotherhood in men in this world.

In the context of this analysis of the divinised humanity, developing the universality in man, we may examine the integral approach of Sri Aurobindo to his idea of the religion of Man as the religion of *Superman or Superhuman*. This is the fundamental Truth of life and existence, in the context of which there is an evolution of human nature which is not concerned with man as he exists or as he appears as the physical aggregates in the last stage of worldly evolution. But it is concerned with the evolution of human nature or inner states of consciousness that leads to the development of Man, what he shall be and with reference to this idea there will be an evolution of the idea of religion as the natural expression of human nature which finally leads to the expression of the universal or infinite nature of Man as the religion of *Superman or Superhuman*.

In the background of this analysis, the meaning of religion transcends the limits of different types of religions and thus it does not mean the imposition of ideas or something on the essential development of man; but it, on the other hand, is eternally related with the expression and realisation of Man in Man. In this context, it is to be noted that religion is not mere individual realisation or realisation of moral, social, cultural or human values in society for the fulfillment of particular purpose as advocated by different types of religious, ethical, sociological or philosophical thoughts. But Sri Aurobindo points out that religion as the religion of Man must have a wider, integral approach that must have a cosmic purpose for the cosmic realisation of Reality in different degrees as the realisation of higher values in different forms, expressing the different states of freedom towards the expression of highest state of freedom in unity through which there will be the inauguration of the religion of *Superman or Superhuman* and thus there will be the expression of universality or infiniteness as divinity in individual and finally in the collective or social existence of men leading to the divine life on earth.

So in the introduction of the religion of *Superman or Superhuman* there will be the introduction of the divine value in individual and social existence of man in the background of the transcendental value as Divine Reality.

It works in the following manner:

(a) In the context of the highest value of Reality, there will be the transcendence of different limitations in individual existence through which man exists as self-transcending being.

(b) This process of transcendence in social existence of man leads to the transcendence of different contradictions or evils in society.

(c) Again this process makes different values free from their limited approaches and thus there will be a transvaluation of values in different degrees.

It should be noted here that the fundamental object of this process is not to transcend this life and world, but to make these states more significant through the transcendence of limitedness or finiteness in different stages for the introduction of unity, manifested in the highest state of human freedom in unity through the realisation of divine unity as the highest human value of divinised humanity, the realisation as experiential process of which makes man Universal, expressing divine life in this world.

This process of transcendence, transformation and unification, according to Sri Aurobindo, is a process of reconciliation of contradictions or limitations in unity, which is neither mere individual or material, nor mere social but is a creative synthesis in the spiritual process of divine union or *Yoga* through which there will be an inauguration of divinity in man and society leading to the development of man as *Superman*, introducing divine life on earth.

But this idea of developing *Superman or Superhuman* in the individual existence, may be treated by some thinkers as superhuman and supernatural development which may be compared with the Nietzsche's idea of *Superman* as Asuric or Titanic man.

It should be noted in this connection, that though Nietzsche and Sri Aurobindo emphasise the advancement of human race towards higher level, Sri Aurobindo does not accept it as the development of physical strength for acquiring material pleasure or demonic power to rule, it, on the other hand, is the development of inner spirit but the harmonious development of material, social and spiritual existence as the expression of divinity in man. The development of the inner spirit for the inauguration of divinity in human existence, according to Sri Aurobindo, is the emergence of *Superman or Superhuman* in the process of evolution which is Ascent and Descent or Involution of the spirit. This spiritual progress is not an abstract development, devoid of materiality and again its emphasis is not over the expression of mere spiritual Reality, but it, on the other hand, is the synthesis of materiality and spirituality, developing the Gnostic Being or God-Man in the human existence. This development means the realisation of godness as the highest human value of divinity united with humanity, expressed integrally in highest state of human freedom in unity. In this context of analysis, Rabindranath also takes Sri Aurobindo's Supermind as the human mind and the realisation of Life Divine also is taken by him as the accomplished man of the highest state of human value as unity or non-duality as *Advaitam.* This spirit of non-duality, according to Tagore, is the expression of the universal nature of man as the real religion of Man, manifesting the 'divinity of man' and the 'humanity of God', that influences Sri Aurobindo to evaluate this idea as "A glint of the greater Era of man's living something that seems to be in promise."[4]

Now it may be said in this connection, that Sri Aurobindo's idea of the religion of Man as the Gnostic development of God-Man as *Superman or Superhuman* is the realisation of highest human value of divinised humanity, manifesting the highest state of human freedom in unity. But it should be noted here that this idea of human freedom is not the realisation of divinity in individual man in leading to individual salvation, but Sri Aurobindo's idea of freedom is the universal idea, expressing the divinity of mankind which finally makes the divine life on earth possible. Professor Maitra writes thus: "The path of individual salvation is the path favoured by a long tradition in our country. But Sri Aurobindo is decidedly of opinion that this path is not enough, as it cannot lead to a total transformation of nature, a radical change in the universe, which is, however, what we need. In spite of there having been so many emancipated souls, so many *Jeevanmukta Purusas*, the world is groping in the dark as much as before. It is clear, therefore, that the production of a few or even a large number of emancipated beings has not produced any permanent improvement of the world. What is necessary for its ideal, radical and permanent improvement is the descent of the Supermind into Earth-Consciousness."[5]

This 'descent of the Supermind into Earth-Consciousness' means the transformation of worldly nature leading to the development of the universal form of human freedom, expressing divinity in the individual and social states of existence in the world. In this highest state of human freedom through the expression of the divinised humanity in love and service of mankind, man is intimately related with others and thus manifests his universal nature, free from limitation and contradiction as the ordinary bondages of life, due to poor ego or individual interest. This human process, according to Sri Aurobindo, finally leads to the spiritual process of divine union or *Yoga*, revealing a synthesis of material, mental, social and spiritual relations, manifesting a divine unity in all.

In this context of the analysis of the nature of human freedom, revealing the universal nature of man, Sri Aurobindo's idea may be compared with the existentialistic approach to the freedom of man. J. P. Sartre, a great Existentialist, also points out that the bondage of life lies in contradiction between individual and social existence and man becomes free from this bondage through the realisation of infiniteness in his finite existence, revealing his universal nature, expressed through unity with others in society. In '*The Problem of Method*', Sartre evaluates this human outlook of social freedom: '...in thus willing freedom, we discover that it depends entirely upon the freedom of others and that the freedom of others depends upon our own.' So in the analysis of human freedom, Existentialists observe the unity of individual and social existence of man, revealing his infiniteness or universality, which, in their observations, is nothing but his social nature, revealed through the social freedom in unity in the realisation of social value of humanity.

In the background of this evaluation of human existence and human freedom, Sri Aurobindo may also be regarded as Existentialist and Humanist, because he deals with the humanistic approach to life that evaluates the proper meaning of existence, revealing human freedom in unity. But Sri Aurobindo's idea of human existence is not mere material or individual and social, but is a synthesis of all these forms, expressing his universal nature as a self-transcending being through the realisation of the highest value of divinised humanity in the process of divine union or *Yoga*, finally expressed in the freedom in unity that leads to the divine life on earth.

So the existential approach of Sri Aurobindo does not deal with mere individual and social existence of man, which, according to him, is spiritual or divine, who, on one hand, can transcend his finiteness or contradictions and on the other hand, can reconcile this contradictions in unity through the realisation of divinity as the highest human value of divinised humanity.

Thus, Sri Aurobindo's human approach to the divine existence of man, evaluated as the religion of *Superman or Superhuman*, finally introduces spiritual or divinised *Humanism*, which is integral in nature as it, on the one hand, synthesises social, cultural, moral, spiritual and human approaches to existence and this integral approach to human existence, makes Sri Aurobindo's novel programme of divine or integral *Humanism* as unique, which is distinct from the humanistic and absolutistic interpretations of man and *Humanism*.

In the evaluation of the term *Humanism*, it is observed by F.C.S. Schiller that "Humanism in philosophy is opposed to Naturalism and Absolutism".[6] *Naturalism* treats man as the natural event and *Absolutism* also takes man as the expression of idea and thus these thoughts deny the distinctness of human personality. But the modern changes through the introduction of *Neo-Naturalism* and the establishment of the idea of the concrete universal in *Absolutism*, man is not going to be dehumanised. Man, on the other hand, is placed at the centre of thought and world and in this way *Humanism* appears as the compromise of these opposite views where man has a unique existence to express his potential greatness through the realisation of human values. In the context of this analysis of human existence, the idea of *Humanism* in these days appears as anthropocentric or divine. The anthropocentric idea of *Humanism* emphasises the individual or material existence of man as the centre of everything that finally leads to a contradiction of individual or material interest and social interest as the dualism of self and not-self. For this it is treated by Maritain as '*Inhuman Humanism*'.

In the background of this evaluation of the idea of *Humanism*, it is observed that Sri Aurobindo supports the idea of *Spiritual* or *Divinised Humanism* and thus, though he is a humanist, still opposes the idea of *anthropocentric Humanism* and also opposes other views of humanists like Comte, Schiller and others who regard physical, vital or mental man as the final state of evolution and accept this man as the basis of truth. This type of man centred thought, according to Sri Aurobindo, emphasises the limitation or finiteness of man, due to his material or individual '*ego*', satisfying narrow and individual interest that is in contrast with the collective or social interest of men in society. In order to avoid this ego-centric idea of man and *Humanism*, Sri Aurobindo emphasises the social and collective interests of people and inter-personal relationship, developing unity in the world. In this process of development, Sri Aurobindo points out that man is not finite or limited, who is taken as a means of fulfilling some interests, he, on the other hand, is treated as a creative personality, manifesting potential universality in different degrees in different creative stages of life, leading to union. For this, he puts an importance of the universal or infinite spirit in man as God in man, which makes man a self-transcending being who can overcome his limitations or contradictions through the realisation of the Transcendental Reality as the value of divinised humanity leading to the development of the divine life on earth as the manifestation of unity in individual and social life in different stages, expounding creativity or creative unity.

Thus, in the context of this analysis of Sri Aurobindo, man, through the realisation of his universal spirit as the transcendental value of divinity, finally becomes *Superman or Superhuman* beyond any limited and restricted ideas and through the expression of the ideal of divinised humanity in individual and social life, there is the introduction of the *Spiritual* or *Divinised Humanism* on earth which is integral in nature. In the evaluation of *Superman or Superhuman* and *Divinised Humanism*, though Sri Aurobindo appears to be absolute idealist as he emphasises the supreme importance of the idea of Absolute or Ultimate Reality in life and existence, still like other absolutists, he does not take it as abstract idea or static thought, killing creativity in human personality. He, on the other hand, as an intuitionist like Bergson, takes Reality as dynamic that can transcend the limitations in different degrees and thus can be intuitively realised in different stages by an individual as a self-transcending spirit.

In the background of the realisation of this Reality as the spirit of unity or universality in the individual, Sri Aurobindo, as an individualist, accepts the individuality of the physical or the material existence of man; but he, as a spiritual individualist, emphasises the realisation of universality or infiniteness for the transcendence of limitation or finiteness of material existence. This, according to Sri Aurobindo, can lead to the realisation of divinity in man as the inauguration of God in man, when God appears as Supreme Person or *Superman as Superhuman*, but he also stands as Superhuman value of transcendental divinity as Supreme or Infinite Reality, in the background of which the human life and world can realise or experience divinity in different stages in different degrees.

Thus, in the context of this analysis of Sri Aurobindo's idea of the religion of Man as the eternal or natural expression of divinity in human existence as *Superman or Superhuman*, his idea of religion can be treated by Sri Aurobindo as 'A spiritual *religion of humanity* is the hope of the future'. This *religion of humanity*, in the opinion of Sri Aurobindo, '...means the growing realisation that there is a secret Spirit, a divine Reality, in which we are all one,...' The introduction of the spirit of oneness or unity in man and society, is the fundamental object of Sri Aurobindo's idea of the *religion of humanity*, introducing *Spiritual* or *Divinised Humanism*, which, finally evaluated by Sri Aurobindo as "....a growing attempt to live out this knowledge and bring about a kingdom of this divine Spirit upon earth. By its growth within us oneness with our fellow men will become the leading principle of all our life, not merely a principle of co-operation but a deeper brotherhood, a real and an inner sense of unity and equality and a common life".[7]

This humanistic process '....as a growing attempt to live...' maybe treated by Sri Aurobindo as spiritual as 'a real and an inner sense of unity and equality and a common life', and it, in this sense of humanistic development, is examined in the form of expanding *Spiritual Humanism* with a realisation of divinised humanity. It, in his opinion, is dynamic, continuous and comprehensive development of human nature and existence. If we explain the human nature in this sense, we find that this type of humanistic expansion is not passive process of realising some human qualities as expanded in Western concept of *Humanism*. But, Sri Aurobindo's philosophy of *Spiritual Humanism*, on the otherhand, is to be taken as the constructive and creative development of human personality in expounding his potential divinity in material, social, cultural and spiritual states of life and existence in an integral way in leading to the creative development of man as Man, the Universal.

Man, in this process, is purely creative in expanding constructive nature of his existence actively and so man, in developing his supernature becomes *Superman or Superhuman* who is purely creative or *Sristisheel* in nature and form.

In this background, the *Spiritual Humanism* of Sri Aurobindo is to be evaluated in modern sense, as the Theory of Creative Man or *Sristisheel Manavbad* in expounding creative nature of divinity in man with a prospect of developing individual as universal or *Superman as Superhuman* in an active and creative process of developing his collective existence in making the divine life on earth, a reality. So, the spiritual process in this context, is to be examined as creative and humanistic process in active and constructive form of expanding the Theory of Creative Man or *Sristisheel Manavbad.*

References

1. R. N. Tagore, The Religion of Man, p. 43.
2. *Ibid*, pp. 40-41.

3. *Ibid.*, p. 11.
4. Sri Aurobindo and Rabindranath Tagore, Sri Aurobindos Ashram, Pondicherry.
5. S. K. Maitra, The Meeting of The East and The West in Sri Aurobindo's Philosophy, p. 334.
6. *Humanism*, Encyclopaedia of Religion and Ethics, Ed. by Hastings, 1955.
7. Sri Aurobindo and The Mother on Human Unity, p. 26.

Chapter - 4

Concluding Observatons: Global Prospect of Expounding Sri Aurobindo's Integral Vision of Humanity

Integral Vision of Humanity

An evaluation of the teleological progress of Sri Aurobindo's life and thought proves the synthesis of the idea and the existence as the expression of the religion of his life that denounces the traditional view of religion as the imposition of idea on existence. It, according to Sri Aurobindo, is not an imposition but is a natural expression of human life that properly examines the Indian way of life, standing on its religious outlook. This idea of religion as the natural expression of life and existence is the fundamental basis of Indian thought from which the new and progressive outlook of the contemporary Indian thinkers is evolved for a proper explanation of purpose, procedure and significance of the idea of religion as the natural expression and development of human life.

In the background of this Indian thought and its progressive influence on the contemporary Indian philosophy, Sri Aurobindo develops his integral outlook for an integral evaluation of human nature, expressed through his integral approach to philosophy and religion as the philosophy of religion that centres round the idea of man and thus develops human outlook of religion as the religion of Man.

In the analysis of this idea of the religion of Man, Sri Aurobindo tries to evaluate the proper meaning of religion as human and integral. This integral and humanistic outlook of religion is nothing but the natural expression of human nature, taken as the proper religion of life, which, according to Sri Aurobindo, is an integral development of human nature and existence.

For the explanation of the nature and significance of the integral development of man as his proper religion, Sri Aurobindo examines the evolution of human life, manifesting different human qualities in different stages of life. With the evolution of human life, manifesting different qualities, Sri Aurobindo observes that there is also an evolution of religions, developing these different types of qualities in human life in different ways.

Through a critical enquiry into this evolution of life and evolution of different religions, Sri Aurobindo, in one hand, transcends the limited approach to life, expressing particular quality through a particular process as a particular religion of the world, and he also, on the other hand, through the transcendence of this limitedness, expresses the wider meaning of the religion of life, which is in contrast with different limited approaches by different religions, creating artificialities in the natural expressions and development of human life. The creation of this artificiality in the natural expression of human existence, according to Sri Aurobindo, is to introduce *religionism* or limitation in the natural expression or the religion of life, which, in his opinion, is to be removed for the explanation of the natural and integral development of man and in the evolution of his life. So, religion, in this context, is the natural and harmonious expression of human nature, revealing the fundamental end of human existence above all limitations, customs, creeds etc., which is to be examined by Sri Aurobindo thus: "…the aim of religion, -but not unhappily of creeds and churches–is to further the great aim of Nature by pushing man towards evolution."[1]

In the context of this analysis, Sri Aurobindo examines the different stages of the evolution of human life as the harmonious expression of the different states of human existence for a proper evaluation of the true and the intrinsic nature of man. For this evaluation, Sri Aurobindo puts a less importance on the material and mechanistic approach to the idea of evolution that explains the material existence of man as the final state of expressing individual and social states of life, expressed through different mechanical and artificial relations.

As man is something more than material and mechanical aggregates, Sri Aurobindo explains the evolution of human nature as teleological and spiritual progress which is the integral development of external and internal states of existence. The fundamental object of this spiritual idea of evolution is to explain different inner states of human nature, leading to the highest state of universality or infiniteness in man, expressing eternal and human relation with others in society.

So the evolution of man, according to Sri Aurobindo, is the evolution of different states of inner existence, leading to the expression of universality. Thus it may be observed that the evolution of man is the natural expression of the inner states of man as the essential religion of Man, leading to the final expression of universality as the religion of Universal Man. In the analysis of this evolution of the final state of universality, Sri Aurobindo evaluates the two fundamental forms of human existence as the self-transcending being and as the integral being. The first form of man proves that as man exists in this material world, he exists with the contradictions, arising out of a contrast of individual interests with social or universal interests of life; but he can transcend these contradictions or evils in developing universality in his inner nature and existence. This type of the development of universality, according to Sri Aurobindo, is the self-transcendence or the transcendence of ego or individual interest, responsible for producing evils in social life. But this type of transcendence is not the rejection of contradictions in life and world, but is a reconciliation of contradictions in unity, developing final form of integral existence of Universal Man.

So the spiritual progress of universality in the human existence, firstly, is the transcendence of limitation or finiteness as *ego*, responsible for producing evils in society; secondly, is the transformation of mere individual or material nature as finiteness or *ego* of man into infiniteness or universality that finally ends in synthesis as the unification of materiality or individuality, sociality and spirituality.

This type of spiritual progress as the transcendence, transformation and unification, according to Sri Aurobindo, is nothing but the reconciliation of finiteness or contradiction in unity, developing universality or infiniteness in human existence, which is neither mere material nor mental, nor mere social, but is a creative synthesis, developed through the spiritual process or method of divine union or *Yoga*.

In the analysis of this spiritual process of divine union for the development of unity in human existence, Sri Aurobindo explains its significance as the introduction of religion of Man which is not an imposition of something on man but as the realisation of universality, expressed through the realisation of different human values in experiential process of manifesting different states of the highest value of divine unity as the final expression of the Transcendental Reality. So the realisation of Reality, according to Sri Aurobindo, is the self-realisation of man's own universality, revealing his self-transcending nature in different stages of the expression of human values of love, service and goodness in different stages, leading to the harmonious development of the infinite existence of man as the highest state of divine unity of the materiality and transcendentality.

This type of evaluation, in one hand, is the transcendence of different limited approaches to life which are nothing but the transvaluation of values in different degrees, that, on the other hand, is for the realisation of the highest value of unity as the introduction of divinity in man and world as the inauguration of the *Superman or Superhuman* in human existence, leading to the introduction of the divine life on earth, manifesting the highest state of human freedom, in the expression of eternal and intimate relation of unity with all.

So the idea of the religion of Man as the realisation of divinity as the highest value, transcending the limitations of different approaches to life, and synthesising all human values, finally leads to the development of *Superman or Superhuman* in human existence for the introduction of unity in life and existence. This idea of developing *Superman or Superhuman*, according to Sri Aurobindo, is the realisation of the inner spirit of universality for the harmonious development of material, social and spiritual states of existence in the process of spiritual evolution in expressing divinity as the Ascent and Descent or Involution of Universal Spirit. Sri Aurobindo's idea of spiritual progress of life and existence is not an abstract improvement without materiality and is not also a mere expression of Abstract Reality or the Absolute, but is a concrete and creative synthesis of materiality, sociality and spirituality as the Gnostic development of Man as God Man or *Superman as Superhuman*. This type of the development of God Man is the introduction of godness as the integral value of divinity and humanity as the divinised humanity, expressed through the eternal and intimate relation with others, which, according to Sri Aurobindo, is a divine union, manifested in the highest state of human freedom in unity. So this idea of the Gnostic development of God Man or *Superman as Superhuman*, through a perfect realisation of divinised humanity in the state of human freedom in unity, thus can be recognised as the human end or ideal, realised through the human method that is for the introduction of unity in human life. For this, Sri Aurobindo's idea of the Gnostic development of *Superman or Superhuman*, is not unnatural and supernatural or development, but it is the extension of inner universal Spirit in human existence, expressed through the human method of love with service of the mankind, which, according to Sri Aurobindo, is the realisation of divinised humanity for the development of intimate or human relation, introducing the Life Divine as the accomplishment of life and existence in the state of freedom.

Thus, it may be pointed out that this idea of human freedom as the realisation of divinised humanity in human existence for the introduction of unity, is not mere the unity of different states of individual existence, leading to the salvation of individual; but it, on the other hand, is also an introduction of unity in the states of collective or social life as the freedom or salvation of mankind as essentially related with the salvation of the individual. So Sri Aurobindo's humanistic approach to the idea of salvation thus leads to the introduction of unity in the external and internal states of individual and social existence and thus finally unites individuality and sociality of life and existence, that, according to Sri Aurobindo, is the development of spirituality as the realisation of the integral value of divinised humanity, leading to the inauguration of the divine life on earth as the final salvation or freedom of mankind.

So this type of humanistic attitude of Sri Aurobindo to the idea of spirituality and again his spiritual approach to the idea of humanity, develop his integral ideal of divinised humanity, expressed through the integral development of the social and spiritual life of men in this world which is the expression of human freedom in unity as the expression of divine life on earth. This expression of the integral existence of man in the integral development of divine unity in the state of freedom, according to Sri Aurobindo, is the eternal and essential expression of the human nature as his religion of Man, which, in his observation, finally leads to the expression of the religion of *Superman or Superhuman*. This idea of the inauguration of *Superman as Superhuman* or God Man in human existence is the expression of godness or divinity in man, which, according to Sri Aurobindo, is an integral expression of values of divinity and humanity in human life. This may be recognised as Sri Aurobindo's humanistic approach to the idea of God or Spirituality, developing the integral ideal of divinised humanity, which finally introduces his idea of the *Spiritual* or *Divinised Humanism*.

In the integral development of the idea of the *Spiritual Humanism*, Sri Aurobindo, as spiritual humanist, synthesises the humanistic and spiritualistic approaches to human existence, which, according to him, is the synthesis of materiality, sociality and spirituality. In the analysis of Sri Aurobindo's idea of the religion of Man as the inauguration of *Superman or Superhuman* in human existence, it is observed that the individual man becomes Universal as *Superman or Superhuman* through the development of his potent universal spirit as the realisation of the transcendental value of divinity, expressed as humanity that is the integral expression of divinised humanity in individual and social life in leading to the introduction of the ideal of Divinised or *Spiritual Humanism*. In the development of this integral ideal, Sri Aurobindo, in one hand, puts an importance on the humanistic approach to life and thus accepts the individuality of man as physical or material existence, but he, on the other hand, ignores the contradictions or evils, caused by the development of mere individuality of man as his finiteness. For this he denies the importance of the individual or man-centred *Humanism* as *anthropocentric Humanism* and finally puts an emphasis on the deeper significance of the individuality of man as the creative personality that is the creative synthesis of humanity and divinity, expressed through the realisation of the divinised humanity in different creative activities of men in different degrees in developing divine unity with all in different stages, towards the introduction of the final state of freedom in unity.

So the inner meaning of the *Spiritual Humanism* as developed by Sri Aurobindo, in his idea of the religion of Man as the inauguration of *Superman or Superhuman* in human existence, is the harmonious development of individual and social states of existence, transcending all limitations and contradictions like different individual and social evils. This idea of *Humanism* as the harmonious advancement of human existence towards completeness, according to Sri Aurobindo, is the eternal and essential expression of human nature as the proper religion of life and existence. This idea of religion as the religion of Man, expressing *Humanism*, is evaluated by Dr Radhakrishnan thus: "It is an age of *Humanism*. Religions which are insensitive to human ills and social crimes do not appeal to the modern man. Religions which make for division, discord and disintegration and do not foster unity, understanding and coherence, play into the hands of the opponents of religion."[2] In the background of this observation, it may be noted that Sri Aurobindo, a great contemporary Indian thinker, develops the inner meaning of spirituality in his idea of religion which is the harmonious development of human life as the synthesis of individuality or materiality, sociality and spirituality which is the introduction of divinity in life and existence as the reconciliation of all contradictions in unity. This eternal spirit of unity in man, emphasises the infiniteness or the universality in him that determines his creative nature in the history of human existence, overcoming different contradictions in life and thus the development of his universal spirit in life and existence finally expresses the deepness or significance of unity in social existence that ascertains the intrinsic nature of socio-moral, socio-economic, socio-political and socio-cultural relations of men, manifesting creative unity as the constructive expression of divine life in the worldly existence. Dr Radhakrishnan thus rightly observes, "A spiritual fellowship is the meaning of history. The purpose of the cosmic process is the city of God in and out of time. Earth is the seed ground of the new life of spirit. Earth and heaven are intermingled."[3]

This idea of expanding 'spiritual fellowship' in the observation of Sri Aurobindo, is the expansion of divinised humanity in expanding the philosophy of *Spiritual Humanism.* This philosophy, in modern sense, is creative and constructive process of developing Man in man as *Superman or Superhuman* who is purely creative or *Sristisheel.* So, the philosophy of Man in this context, is a creative synthesis of divinity and humanity in human existence in leading to the development of the Theory of Creative Man or *Sristisheel Manavbad.* Man, in this humanistic process, is active, constructive and creative and thus expands different states of his existence in creative form, finally develops his collective existence as human freedom and it, according to Sri Aurobindo, is the expansion of the divine life on earth. This process of life as evaluated by Dr Radhakrishnan, is purely creative and humanistic, where 'Earth and heaven are intermingled'.

References

1. Religion–Aim and Nature, Sri Aurobindo and The Mother on Religion, p. 1.
2. Dr S Radhakrishnan, Religion and Culture, pp. 8-9.
3. *Ibid*, p. 9.

A Select Bibliography

Works of Sri Aurobindo

Sri Aurobindo and the Mother on Religion, Sri Aurobindo Society, Pondicherry 2, 1972.

Sri Aurobindo and the Mother on Human Unity, Sri Aurobindo Society, Pondicherry 2, 1973.

Sri Aurobindo and the Mother on The Future of Society, Sri Aurobindo Society, Pondicherry 2, 1973.

Sri Aurobindo and the Mother on Supermind, Sri Aurobindo Society, Pondicherry 2, 1973.

Sri Aurobindo, Collected Poems and Plays, Vol. I.

Sri Aurobindo, The Secret of the Veda, 1971.

Sri Aurobindo, Isha Upanishad, 1973.

Sri Aurobindo, Life Divine, I and II, 1973.

Sri Aurobindo, The Ideal of Human Unity, 1950.

Sri Aurobindo, The Human Cycle, 1949.

Sri Aurobindo, Heraclitus, 1947.

Sri Aurobindo, Essays on The Gita, Vol. I and Vol. II, Calcutta, 1942.

Sri Aurobindo, The Synthesis of *Yoga*, 1955.

Sri Aurobindo, The *Superman*, 1968.

Sri Aurobindo, The Riddle of this World, 1969.

Sri Aurobindo, The Supermental Manifestation, 1949.

Sri Aurobindo, On Himself, compiled from Notes and Letters, 1972.

Sri Aurobindo, Letters of Sri Aurobindo I Series, 1950, II Series, 1949, III Series, 1949, IV Series, 1951.

Sri Aurobindo, Lights on *Yoga*, 1953.

Sri Aurobindo, Ideals and Progress, 1946.

Sri Aurobindo, The Mother, 1940.

Sri Aurobindo, The Upanishads, Texts, Translations and Commentaries, 1972.

Sri Aurobindo, The Renaissance in India, 1946.

Sri Aurobindo, The Foundation of Indian Culture, 1953.

Sri Aurobindo, Man–Slave or Free? 1972.

Sri Aurobindo, More Lights on *Yoga*, 1948.

Sri Aurobindo, Thoughts and Glimpses, 1950.

Sri Aurobindo, The Problem of Re-birth, 1969.

Works on Sri Aurobindo

Srinivasa Iyengar, K R, Sri Aurobindo, Arya Publishing House, Calcutta, 1945.

Purani, A B, The Life of Sri Aurobindo, (1872-1926), Sri Aurobindo Ashram, Pondicherry.

Maitra, S K, Studies in Sri Aurobindo's Philosophy, Benaras Hindu University, 1945.

Maitra, S K, The Meeting of The East and The West in Sri Aurobindo's Philosophy, Sri Aurobindo Ashram, Pondicherry, 1968.

Maitra, S K, An Introduction to the Philosophy of Sri Aurobindo, Sri Aurobindo Ashram, Pondicherry, 1965.

Pearson, N, Sri Aurobindo and the Soul Quest of Man, George Allen & Unwin Ltd., London, 1952.

Keshavmurti, Sri Aurobindo: The Hope of Man, Dipti Publications, Sri Aurobindo Ashram, Pondicherry, 1969.

Chatterjee, Dr P B, Towards *Supermanhood:* The Philosophy of Sri Aurobindo, Progressive Publishers, Calcutta, 1977.

Nedumpalakunnel, C M F, George, Realisation of God according to Sri Aurobindo, Claretian Publications, Bangalore, 1979.

Chattopadhyay, D P, Sri Aurobindo on Man, Sri Aurobindo Pathamandir, Calcutta, 1972.

Anirvan, Divyajivan Prasanga, (Bengali), Sri Aurobindo Ashram, Pondicherry, 1971.

Das, A C, Sri Aurobindo and the Future of Mankind, 1935.

Other Works

Nagaraja Rao, P, Contemporary Indian Philosophy, Bharatiya Vidya Bhavan, Chowpatty: Bombay, 1970.

Srivastava, R S, Contemporary Indian Philosophy, Munshi Ram Manohar Lal, Delhi 6, 1965.

Verma, V P, The Political Philosophy of Sri Aurobindo (2nd Edn), Motilal Banarasidas, Delhi, 1976.

Ward, J, Nationalism and Agnosticism, 3rd Edn., 1906.

Comte, A, General View of Positivism, translated by Bridges, J H, Trubner & Co., London, 1865.

Barnett, L, The Universe and Dr Einstein, 1950.

Huxley, Sir J, Evolution after Darwin, Vol. III.

Tagore, R N, The Religion of Man, Unwin Books, London, 1970.

Bradley, F H, Appearance and Reality, Ninth Impression, Clarendon Press, Oxford.

Alexander, S, Space Time Deity, Vol. I and II, 1920.

Radhakrishnan, Dr S, Religion and Culture, An Orient Paperback, India.

Dutta, D M, The Chief Currents of Contemporary Philosophy, The University of Calcutta, 1961.

Teilhard de Chardin, The Phenomenon of Man, 1959.

Haldane, J B S, The Marxist Philosophy and The Sciences, London, 1939.

Dasgupta, S N, Hindu Mysticism, Frederick Ungarn Publishing Co., New York, 1971.

Hiriyana, M, Outlines of Indian Philosophy, George Allen & Unwin, London, 1970.

Underhill, E, The Essentials of Mysticism and Other Essays, J M Dent & Sons Ltd., London, Toronto, 1920.

Sinha, D, Phenomenology and Existentialism, Progressive Publishers, Calcutta, 1974.

Lewis, H D, Our Experience of God, George Allen & Unwin, London, 1959.

James, Comparative Religion, Mathuen, 1938.

Eddington, Science and the Unseen World, 1929.

Gandhi, M K, My Religion, Navaranjan, Ahmedabad, 1958.

Radhakrishnan, S, Indian Philosophy, George Allen & Unwin, London, 1931.

Radhakrishnan, S, The Creative Life, Orient Paperbacks, India, 1975.

Blackham, Six Existentialist Thinkers, R & K Paul Ltd., London, 1961.

Bosanquet, B, The Principle of Individuality and Value, Macmillan, London, 1927.

Chatterjee, P B, Studies in Comparative Religion, Calcutta, 1971.

Das, A C, A Modern Incarnation of God, G P & P Ltd., Calcutta, 1958.

Dutta, D M, The Philosophy of Mahatma Gandhi, The University of Calcutta, 1968.

Hartmann, N, Ethics (All Vols.), Allen & Unwin, 1950.

Huxley, A, The Perennial Philosophy, London, 1947.

Jaspers, A, The Future of Mankind, Chicago, 1961.

Ducasse, C J, A Philosophical Scrutiny of Religion, Rona Press, 1953.

Martineau, J, A Study of Religion: Its Sources and Contents, 2nd Edn., Clarendon Press, Oxford, 1926.

Marx, K, and Engles, F, Selected Works (In 1 Vol.), Moscow, Russia, 1970.

Pattison, P, Seth, A, The Idea of God in the Light of Recent Philosophy, 2nd Edn., 1967, (Reprint).

Rolland, R, Swami Vivekananda, Translated by E F Malcolm Smith, Advaita Ashram, Almora.

Seal, B N, Comparative Studies in Vaishnavism and Christianity, 1899.

Sinha, J N, Moral Idealism and Theism, Jadunath Sinha Foundation, Calcutta, 1978.

Moore, G E, Some Main Problems of Philosophy, London, 1962.

Moore, G E, Principia Ethica, Cambridge University Press, 1965.

Roy, S, Bharater Baiplavik Sangramer Itihas (Bengali), Vol. I, PNBA Brothers, Calcutta, 1970.

Sen, K M, Bharater Sanskriti (Bengali), Visvabharati, Calcutta, 1352. B. A.

MacIver, R M, and Page, C H, Society, London, 1962.

Bhadra, M K, A Critical Study of Sartre's Ontology of Consciousness, The University of Burdwan, 1978.

The Edited Works

Chattopadhyay, S N, The World Peace, Punthipustak, Kolkata, 2005.

Chattopadhyay, S N, Freedom, Naya Prokash, Calcutta, 1996.

Saint–Hilare, P B, Sri Aurobindo: The Future Evolution of Man, Sri Aurobindo Ashram, Pondicherry, India, 1974.

Hastings, Encyclopaedia of Religion and Ethics, Vol. VI, T & T Clark, Edinburgh, 1955.

Encyclopaedia of Britannica, Vols. II, XI, Encyclopaedia Britannica, Inc, William Benton, 1969.

Sri Aurobindo and Rabindranath Tagore, Sri Aurobindo Ashram, Pondicherry, India, 1961.

Mahadevan, T M P and Cairns, G E, Contemporary Indian Philosophers of History, World Press, Calcutta.

Radhakrishnan, S, and Muirhead, J H, Contemporary Indian Philosophy, Allen and Unwin, London, 1956.

Solomon, R C, Phenomenology and Existentialism, Harper & Row, 1972.

Mohanty, J N, and Banerjee, S P, Self Knowledge and Freedom, World Press, Calcutta, 1978.

Ryazanskaya, S, The German Ideology–Karl Marx & Frederick Engles, Moscow, 1964.

Cornford, F M, The Republic of Plato, Clarendon Press, Oxford, 1961.

Cultural Heritage of India, The Ramkrishna Mission Institute of Culture, Calcutta (Reprinted 1917).

Paton, H J, The Moral Law: Kant's Ground Work of The Meta Physic of Morals, London, 1972.

Some Journals and Souvenirs

Karmayogin, Number VIII.

Sri Aurobindo Mandir Annual, Vol. II.

Sri Aurobindo Mandir Annual, No. 6, August, 1947.

Visvabharati Quarterly, Vol. XVIII, 1953.

Sri Aurobindo Janma Satavarsiki Smarak Grantha, Sri Aurobindo Pathamandir, Calcutta, 15th August, 1972.

Betar Jagat, Calcutta (16th–31st August, 1980).

Sri Aurobindo Smarane, Bidyutchakra Sadharan Pathagar, Dum Dum, Calcutta, 1972.

The Advent, Vol. XI, No. 2.

Sri Aurobindo Circle Annual, 12th Issue.

The World Union, Pondicherry (1980-81).

The Arya (1914-1921).

Bandemataram, (1907-1908).